TROTSKY

DATE DUE

TROTSKY

A GRAPHIC BIOGRAPHY by Rick Geary

A NOVEL GRAPHIC from HILL AND WANG

A division of FARRAR, STRAUS AND GIROUX   NEW YORK

Hill and Wang
A division of Farrar, Straus and Giroux
18 West 18th Street, New York 10011

Serious Comics GNC, LLC
621 East 11th Street, New York 10009

Distributed in Canada by D&M Publishers, Inc.
Printed in the United States of America
First edition, 2009

Library of Congress Cataloging-in-Publication Data
Geary, Rick.
    Trotsky : a graphic biography / Rick Geary.—1st ed.
        p. cm.
    Includes bibliographical references.
    ISBN-13: 978-0-8090-9508-7 (pbk. : alk. paper)
    ISBN-10: 0-8090-9508-4 (pbk. : alk. paper)
    1. Trotsky, Leon, 1879–1940—Comic books, strips, etc. 2. Revolutionaries—Soviet
Union—Biography—Comic books, strips, etc. 3. Statesmen—Soviet Union—Biography—
Comic books, strips, etc. 4. Exiles—Russia—Biography—Comic books, strips, etc.
5. Communism—Soviet Union—Comic books, strips, etc. 6. Russia—Politics and
government—1894–1917—Comic books, strips, etc. 7. Soviet Union—Politics and
government—1917–1936—Comic books, strips, etc. 8. Graphic novels. I. Title.

DK254.T6G43 2009
947.084092—dc22
[B]
                                                                            2008050235

Produced by Jessica Marshall, Ph.D., and Andrew J. Helfer
Lettering by Dan Nakrosis

www.fsgbooks.com

1 3 5 7 9 10 8 6 4 2

CONTENTS

Part 1: A YOUNG REVOLUTIONARY · 3

Part 2: PRISON AND EXILE · 15

Part 3: THE YEAR 1905 · 27

Part 4: PRISON AND EXILE AGAIN · 35

Part 5: THE YEAR 1917 · 49

Part 6: A NEW NATION · 63

Part 7: FALL FROM POWER · 77

Part 8: THE FINAL EXILE · 87

Further Reading · *103*

TROTSKY

PART ☭ ONE
A YOUNG REVOLUTIONARY

IN 1917, LEON TROTSKY BURST UPON THE INTERNATIONAL STAGE AS THE BRAIN BEHIND THE RUSSIAN REVOLUTION. HE PRESIDED OVER THE COMPLETE TRANSFORMATION OF HIS COUNTRY, NOT MERELY A CHANGE OF GOVERNMENT BUT A TOTAL RESTRUCTURING OF SOCIETY ON EVERY LEVEL.

TO MANY, HE WAS THE HEROIC ST. GEORGE, SLAYING THE DRAGON OF CAPITALIST REPRESSION.

TO OTHERS, HE WAS THE RUTHLESS AND SATANIC PURVEYOR OF BLOODY REBELLION, THE COLD, DETACHED THEORIST GONE MAD WITH POWER.

IN TRUTH, HE FITTED NEITHER OF THESE IMAGES. HE WAS A WRITER, A THINKER, AND A NATION BUILDER—ALBEIT A RELUCTANT ONE—WITH DEEP ROOTS IN HIS RUSSIA'S AGRICULTURAL HEARTLAND.

TROTSKY'S DREAM WAS FOR A WORLD FREE FROM INJUSTICE, INEQUALITY, AND WAR, AND IN THIS HE WAS ABSOLUTELY SINGLE-MINDED.

TO HIM, THE IDEAS OF KARL MARX SHOWED THE WAY, AND FOR ONE BRIEF MOMENT HE SET THE MACHINERY IN MOTION TO ACHIEVE THAT END.

BUT IN SO DOING, HE SET UP A WORLD CONFLICT THAT LASTED THROUGHOUT THE CENTURY.

HE LIVED TO SEE HIS WORK BETRAYED AND HIS IDEALS PERVERTED BY THOSE WHO SEIZED POWER AFTER HIM. HE WOULD BE EJECTED FROM THE GOVERNMENT HE HELPED TO ESTABLISH AND HOUNDED INTO EXILE AND DEATH.

4

IN 1879, THE RUSSIAN EMPIRE WAS A VAST LAND THAT STRETCHED FROM EUROPE, ACROSS ASIA, TO THE PACIFIC OCEAN...

☆ ST. PETERSBURG

◉ MOSCOW

◉ KIEV

...UNDER ITS ABSOLUTE RULER, TSAR ALEXANDER II.

THE PEASANTS WORKED THE LAND IN A FEUDAL SYSTEM THAT HAD NOT CHANGED IN CENTURIES...

...WHILE FACTORY WORKERS IN THE OVERCROWDED URBAN CENTERS EXPERIENCED THE ECONOMIC PRIVATION THAT ACCOMPANIED THE NATION'S RAPID INDUSTRIALIZATION.

PEASANT REBELLIONS HAD BEEN A PERIODIC FACT OF LIFE IN RUSSIA, GOING BACK AT LEAST TO THE REIGN OF PETER THE GREAT IN THE 17TH CENTURY.

IN THE 1860S, ALEXANDER II USHERED IN AN ERA OF REFORM AND LIBERALIZATION. BUT THIS WAS NOT ENOUGH FOR SOME.

THE TERRORIST PEOPLE'S WILL PARTY INITIATED STRIKES, PROPAGANDA, AND AGITATION THROUGHOUT THE 1870S.

IT ALSO PRONOUNCED A DEATH SENTENCE UPON THE TSAR. THE YEAR 1879 SAW THE FIRST DYNAMITE ASSAULT AGAINST THE MONARCHY, WITH AN UNSUCCESSFUL ATTEMPT UPON THE IMPERIAL TRAIN.

THAT YEAR ALSO SAW THE BIRTH OF THE MAN WHO WOULD EVENTUALLY GUIDE THIS ROUGH AND DISORGANIZED REVOLUTIONARY FERVOR TO FRUITION.

THE MAN WHO WOULD BECOME LEON TROTSKY WAS BORN LEV DAVIDOVICH BRONSTEIN ON OCTOBER 26, 1879*...

☆KIEV

U K R A I N E

...ON A FARM NEAR THE TINY VILLAGE OF YANOVKA IN THE SOUTHERN PROVINCE OF KHERSON, IN THE REGION KNOWN AS THE UKRAINE.

KHERSON

YANOVKA

ODESSA

SEA OF AZOV

BLACK

*A NOTE ABOUT DATES: DURING THIS TIME THE RUSSIAN EMPIRE STILL KEPT TO THE JULIAN CALENDAR, PUTTING IT 13 DAYS BEHIND THE REST OF EUROPE, WHICH HAD GRADUALLY SWITCHED TO THE "NEW" GREGORIAN CALENDAR OVER THE PREVIOUS THREE CENTURIES. FOR THIS NARRATIVE, DATES WILL BE NOTED AS PER THE "OLD" (JULIAN) SYSTEM.

HE WAS THE SECOND OF THE FOUR SURVIVING CHILDREN OF DAVID BRONSTEIN AND HIS WIFE, ANNA.

HIS SIBLINGS: OLDER BROTHER, ALEXANDER; YOUNGER SISTERS, ELIZABETH ("LIZA") AND OLGA.

7

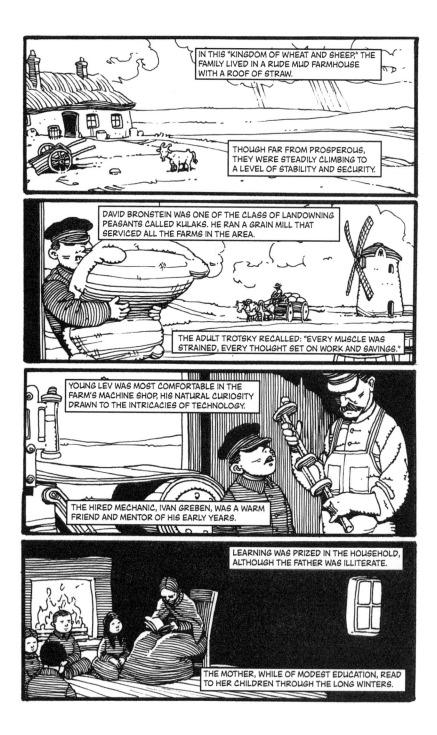

IN THIS "KINGDOM OF WHEAT AND SHEEP," THE FAMILY LIVED IN A RUDE MUD FARMHOUSE WITH A ROOF OF STRAW.

THOUGH FAR FROM PROSPEROUS, THEY WERE STEADILY CLIMBING TO A LEVEL OF STABILITY AND SECURITY.

DAVID BRONSTEIN WAS ONE OF THE CLASS OF LANDOWNING PEASANTS CALLED KULAKS. HE RAN A GRAIN MILL THAT SERVICED ALL THE FARMS IN THE AREA.

THE ADULT TROTSKY RECALLED: "EVERY MUSCLE WAS STRAINED, EVERY THOUGHT SET ON WORK AND SAVINGS."

YOUNG LEV WAS MOST COMFORTABLE IN THE FARM'S MACHINE SHOP, HIS NATURAL CURIOSITY DRAWN TO THE INTRICACIES OF TECHNOLOGY.

THE HIRED MECHANIC, IVAN GREBEN, WAS A WARM FRIEND AND MENTOR OF HIS EARLY YEARS.

LEARNING WAS PRIZED IN THE HOUSEHOLD, ALTHOUGH THE FATHER WAS ILLITERATE.

THE MOTHER, WHILE OF MODEST EDUCATION, READ TO HER CHILDREN THROUGH THE LONG WINTERS.

AT AGE SIX, LEV BEGAN ATTENDING PRIMARY SCHOOL IN THE NEARBY TOWN OF GROMOKLEI.

HERE HE LEARNED TO READ AND WRITE. HE MADE FEW FRIENDS BECAUSE COMING FROM AN UPWARDLY MOBILE JEWISH FAMILY, HE DID NOT SPEAK YIDDISH.

IN 1888, AT AGE NINE, HE WAS SENT TO ODESSA TO STUDY AT THE ST. PAUL REALSCHULE.

THE FARM BOY WAS IMMEDIATELY THRILLED AND SEDUCED BY THE SOPHISTICATED URBAN ENVIRONMENT.

HE LIVED WITH THE FAMILY OF HIS OLDER COUSIN MOISHE SHPENTSER, A CHARISMATIC FREELANCE JOURNALIST, LATER A PUBLISHER.

FROM HIM, TROTSKY LATER RECALLED, THE BOY LEARNED A "LOVE OF THE FRESHLY PRINTED PAGE."

IN SCHOOL HE PROVED HIMSELF AN EXCEPTIONALLY BRIGHT AND CAPABLE STUDENT, ESPECIALLY IN SCIENCE AND ARITHMETIC.

HE WAS BY MOST ACCOUNTS A MODEL PUPIL: OBEDIENT, PROMPT, ATTENTIVE. HE LATER REMEMBERED LIKING NOT A SINGLE TEACHER.

BY HIS OWN ADMISSION, HE WAS MORE CAPTIVATED BY BOOKS AND IDEAS THAN BY PEOPLE AND NATURE.

THESE YEARS MARKED THE BEGINNINGS OF A BREAK WITH HIS FATHER'S VALUES.

DURING LEV'S VISITS HOME FROM ODESSA HE DID THE BOOKKEEPING FOR THE FARM AND MILL. THIS BROUGHT THE DIFFERENCES BETWEEN FARMWORKER AND LANDOWNER INTO SHARP FOCUS.

THE BOY'S NEW SPECTACLES WERE DISAPPROVED OF BY THE OLDER MAN AS AFFECTED...

...BUT LEV FELT THEY GAVE HIM A LOOK OF IMPORTANCE.

THOUGH HE HAD YET TO GAIN A POLITICAL AWARENESS, HE HAD AN INSTINCTIVE SYMPATHY FOR THE PEASANTS IN HIS FATHER'S EMPLOY.

IN DISPUTES HE AUTOMATICALLY TOOK THE SIDE OF THE OPPRESSED.

HE SENSED A RESENTMENT AMONG THE WORKERS THAT WAS TO BLOSSOM INTO AN ANGER SEARCHING FOR RELEASE.

THUS THE YOUNG MAN GREW AWAY FROM HIS FAMILY...

...AND THUS WAS PLANTED IN HIM A SENSE OF TYRANNY AND EXPLOITATION...

...AND OF ENMITY TO THE EXISTING ORDER.

10

THE YEAR 1894 SAW THE DEATH OF TSAR ALEXANDER III AND THE ASCENSION TO THE THRONE OF HIS SON, NICHOLAS II.

THE NEW RULER SAW NO NEED FOR REFORMS OR LIBERALIZATION. THE IDEA OF A CONSTITUTION WAS "NONSENSICAL."

TWO YEARS LATER 17-YEAR-OLD LEV BRONSTEIN COMPLETED HIS STUDIES IN ODESSA AND WAS SENT BY HIS FATHER TO THE PROVINCIAL TOWN OF NIKOLAEV TO PREPARE FOR UNIVERSITY ENTRANCE.

DNIEPER R.

YANOVKA   NIKOLAEV

ODESSA

HIS GOAL AT THAT TIME WAS A DEGREE IN MATHEMATICS AND AN EVENTUAL CAREER IN ENGINEERING.

HE ARRIVED THERE IN THE TRAPPINGS OF PRIVILEGE, A BRILLIANT YOUNG MAN, FULL OF SELF-CONFIDENCE...

...AND PERHAPS A TOUCH OF ARROGANCE.

HIS HEALTH WAS DELICATE. FROM HIS CHILDHOOD, NERVOUS SHOCKS AFFECTED HIS DIGESTION.

HE WAS ALSO SUBJECT TO SPELLS OF FAINTING DURING PERIODS OF STRESS AND ANXIETY.

BUT A TRANSFORMATION OF THE YOUNG MAN'S CONSCIOUSNESS WAS SOON TO OCCUR.

THE TOWN OF NIKOLAEV WAS HOME TO MANY FORMER ACTIVISTS OF THE PEOPLE'S WILL PARTY. AFTER A DECADE'S DORMANCY, TALK OF REVOLUTION WAS AGAIN IN THE AIR.

THE HOME IN WHICH HE BOARDED WAS FILLED WITH YOUNG MEN OF SOCIALIST AND POPULIST LEANINGS.

LEV, WHOSE POLITICAL VIEWS WERE VAGUE AT BEST, ATTEMPTED TO ESCAPE THEIR INFLUENCE, BUT IT WAS A LOSING BATTLE.

AS HE LATER PUT IT, HE "SWUNG LEFTWARD WITH SUCH SPEED THAT IT EVEN FRIGHTENED AWAY SOME OF MY NEW FRIENDS."

HE BECAME IMMERSED IN REVOLUTIONARY STUDIES, AND IT WAS NOT LONG BEFORE HE BEGAN SKIPPING CLASSES AND NEGLECTING HIS SCHOOLWORK.

THE NEW PHILOSOPHY OF MARXISM WAS GAINING IN POPULARITY AMONG THE YOUNG REVOLUTIONARIES. IT OFFERED A FRESH WAY OF VIEWING HISTORY, AS THE PRODUCT OF CONSTANTLY WARRING ECONOMIC FORCES.

KAPITAL

IN THIS VIEW, CAPITALISM WAS A SYSTEM OF REPRESSION AND ENSLAVEMENT THAT WOULD IN TIME SOW THE SEEDS OF ITS OWN DESTRUCTION.

IN 1848 THE GERMAN PHILOSOPHERS KARL MARX AND FRIEDRICH ENGELS HAD ISSUED THEIR *COMMUNIST MANIFESTO*. IT VENTURED BEYOND MERE SOCIALISM, WHICH CALLED ONLY FOR THE COLLECTIVE OWNERSHIP OF THE MEANS OF PRODUCTION...

ENGELS

MARX

...TO THE ABOLITION OF ALL PRIVATE PROPERTY AND THE ESTABLISHMENT OF A WORKERS' STATE— BY VIOLENT MEANS IF NECESSARY. WORKERS OF ALL LANDS, UNITE!

THE SOCIAL DEMOCRATIC LABOR PARTY HAD BEEN ORGANIZED IN GERMANY TO BRING THIS ABOUT, AND ITS RUSSIAN COUNTERPART WAS PROVING ESPECIALLY ATTRACTIVE TO STUDENTS AT THE UNIVERSITIES AND TECHNICAL SCHOOLS.

LEV, HOWEVER, REJECTED THE TENETS OF MARXISM AS DRY, NARROW, AND IMPRACTICAL.

HE BEGAN TO ASSOCIATE WITH A COMMUNE OF RADICAL YOUTH THAT GATHERED AT THE DACHA OF A LOCAL PHILOSOPHER.

DAYS WERE SPENT IN READING AND DEBATING.

THE ONLY YOUNG WOMAN IN THE GROUP WAS ALEXANDRA SOKOLOVSKAYA, A SELF-PROCLAIMED MARXIST.

SHE AND LEV ARGUED IN A WAY THAT UNDERSCORED THEIR MUTUAL ATTRACTION. THOUGH SHE WAS FIVE YEARS OLDER, BEFORE LONG THEY WERE LOVERS.

FED UP WITH HIS SON'S BEHAVIOR, DAVID BRONSTEIN CUT OFF HIS ALLOWANCE.

DEFIANTLY, THE YOUNG MAN MOVED INTO THE COMMUNE. HE LED A SPARTAN LIFE, DRESSED IN WORKERS' GARB, AND SUPPORTED HIMSELF MEAGERLY BY GIVING PRIVATE LESSONS.

MИРЬ

AS THE ADULT TROTSKY LATER REMEMBERED IT, "WE READ WITHOUT METHOD, WE ARGUED WITHOUT RESTRAINT, WE PEERED INTO THE FUTURE PASSIONATELY, AND WERE HAPPY IN OUR OWN WAY."

LEV AND HIS COMRADES FORMED THE SOUTH RUSSIA WORKERS' UNION IN APRIL 1897.

WARY OF CENTRALIZED POWER, THEY ENVISIONED A LOOSE ORGANIZATION OF SMALL AUTONOMOUS CELLS, LINKED ONLY BY THEIR DEDICATION TO THE CAUSE.

HIS ORGANIZATIONAL SKILLS FLOWERED AS HE GAINED PRACTICAL EXPERIENCE IN SOCIALIST ACTION.

A WHIRLWIND OF ENERGY, HE COLLECTED MONEY FOR STRIKE FUNDS, CONDUCTED EDUCATIONAL PROGRAMS, WROTE AND DISTRIBUTED PROPAGANDA, AND TRAVELED BY STEAMER TO ODESSA TO SPREAD THE WORD.

FROM THIS TIME HE ALWAYS DATED THE START OF HIS LITERARY CAREER. HE MOVED FROM PAMPHLETS AND PROCLAMATIONS DUPLICATED ON THE HECTOGRAPH...

...TO ARTICLES AND EDITORIALS FOR THE NEWSPAPER *OUR CAUSE*.

HIS PATH WAS SET AS A WRITER AND REVOLUTIONARY, JUST AS, ON JANUARY 28, 1898, THE TSAR'S GOVERNMENT DECIDED TO CRACK DOWN.

ON THAT DATE MORE THAN 200 ACTIVISTS WERE PLACED UNDER ARREST.

14

PART TWO

PRISON AND EXILE

OLD PRISON, NIKOLAEV

KHERSON PRISON

NEW PRISON, ODESSA

LEV BRONSTEIN WOULD SPEND THE NEXT TWO YEARS OF HIS LIFE IN A SERIES OF PRISONS, AWAITING TRIAL.

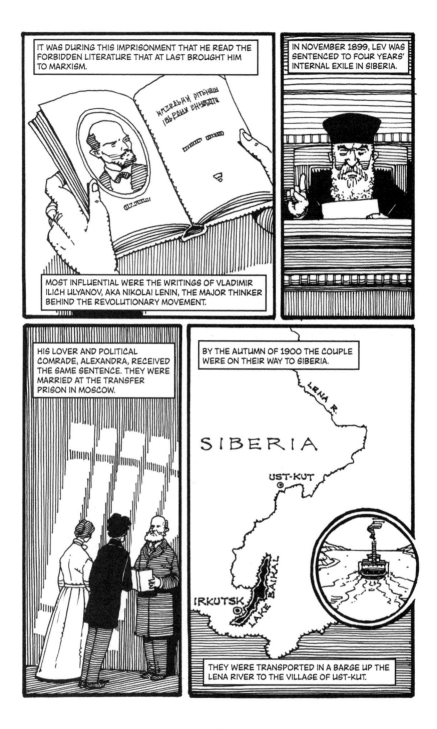

IT WAS DURING THIS IMPRISONMENT THAT HE READ THE FORBIDDEN LITERATURE THAT AT LAST BROUGHT HIM TO MARXISM.

MOST INFLUENTIAL WERE THE WRITINGS OF VLADIMIR ILICH ULYANOV, AKA NIKOLAI LENIN, THE MAJOR THINKER BEHIND THE REVOLUTIONARY MOVEMENT.

IN NOVEMBER 1899, LEV WAS SENTENCED TO FOUR YEARS' INTERNAL EXILE IN SIBERIA.

HIS LOVER AND POLITICAL COMRADE, ALEXANDRA, RECEIVED THE SAME SENTENCE. THEY WERE MARRIED AT THE TRANSFER PRISON IN MOSCOW.

BY THE AUTUMN OF 1900 THE COUPLE WERE ON THEIR WAY TO SIBERIA.

LENA R.

SIBERIA

UST-KUT

IRKUTSK

LAKE BAIKAL

THEY WERE TRANSPORTED IN A BARGE UP THE LENA RIVER TO THE VILLAGE OF UST-KUT.

LIFE WAS DIFFICULT IN THE TINY COMMUNITY OF ABOUT 100 RUDE HUTS.

THE WINTERS BROUGHT SUBZERO TEMPERATURES; THE SUMMERS CARRIED SWARMS OF MOSQUITOES.

COCKROACHES FILLED EVERY HOUSE, MAKING ORDINARY ACTIVITIES DIFFICULT.

NEVERTHELESS, DURING THIS TIME LEV WAS ABLE TO CONTRIBUTE ARTICLES TO A REGIONAL POPULIST NEWSPAPER, *THE EASTERN REVIEW*.

FOR A PEN NAME, HE LIFTED A WORD, *"ANTIDOTO,"* FROM AN ITALIAN DICTIONARY, USING IT TO SIGNIFY THE MARXIST ANTIDOTE TO THE "LIBERAL" PRESS.

AFTER SOME TIME THE COUPLE WERE ALLOWED TO RELOCATE TO A LARGER TOWN, VERKHOLENSK, AND BETTER ACCOMMODATIONS.

THEY PRODUCED TWO DAUGHTERS, ZINAIDA ("ZINA") AND NINA.

IN 1902 THE COUPLE RECEIVED WORD OF A NEW MARXIST NEWSPAPER, *ISKRA* (SPARK), PUBLISHED BY RUSSIAN EXILES IN LONDON, WITH THE GOAL OF CENTRALLY ORGANIZED REVOLUTIONARY ACTION.

YOU MUST!

WITH HIS WIFE'S ENCOURAGEMENT, LEV KNEW THE TIME HAD COME FOR HIS ESCAPE FROM EXILE.

HIS ESCAPE WAS EASILY ENOUGH ARRANGED AND THE STUFF OF MELODRAMA.

FIRST, HE REPORTED SICK TO THE AUTHORITIES, AND HIS BED WAS OCCUPIED BY A FIGURE MADE OF STRAW.

HE LEFT TOWN IN THE BACK OF A PEASANT'S CART, COVERED BY HAY...

LENA R.

IRKUTSK

CHINA

...AND THUS WAS CARRIED SOUTH TO THE TOWN OF IRKUTSK.

THERE HE RECEIVED FRESH CLOTHING AND A NEW PASSPORT, MADE OUT IN THE NAME LEON TROTSKY.

ТРОЦКИЙ, ЛЕВ

HE WROTE THE NAME, HE LATER CLAIMED, TOTALLY AT RANDOM, NEVER IMAGINING THAT IT WOULD BE HIS NAME FOR THE REST OF HIS LIFE.

LEON TROTSKY THEN TRAVELED BY RAIL TO THE CITY OF SAMARA, THERE TO BEGIN, AT AGE 23, HIS NEW LIFE AS A PROFESSIONAL REVOLUTIONARY.

SAMARA

IRKUTSK

SAMARA WAS A MAJOR DISTRIBUTION POINT FOR *ISKRA*...

...AND THERE HE JOINED THE STAFF, WRITING UNDER THE NAME PERO (PEN).

THE REVOLUTIONARY MOVEMENT WAS GROWING, BUT ONLY IN SMALL AND SCATTERED POCKETS.

ПРОЛЕТАРИИ ВСЛЬИБ СТРАНЬ СОЕДИНЯЙТЕСЬ!

ALL IT LACKED WAS A CENTRAL GUIDING AUTHORITY, A UNITY OF THEORY AND PRACTICE.

TO THIS END HE WAS SENT TO A NUMBER OF CITIES, INCLUDING KIEV, KHARKOV, AND POLTAVA...

...TO BRING WAVERING ACTIVISTS INTO THE FOLD.

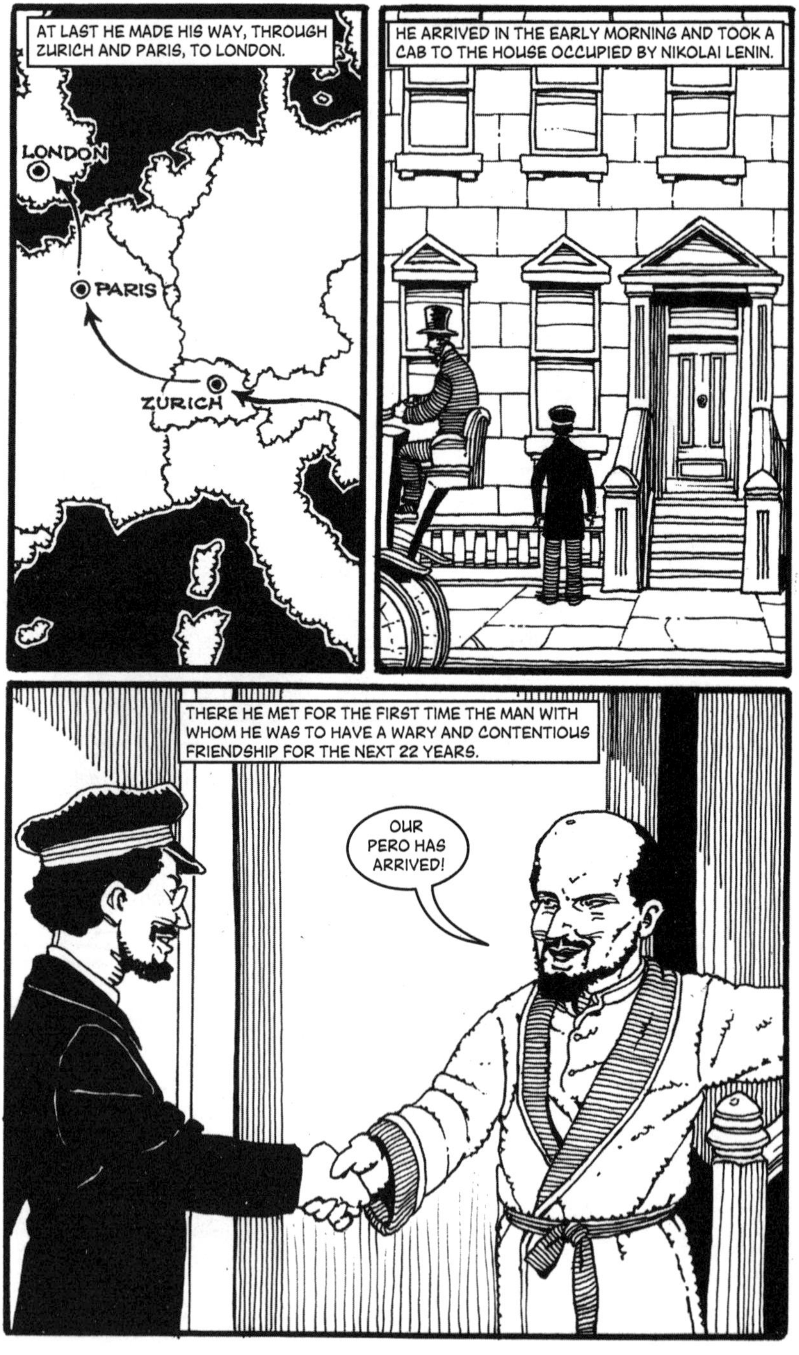
AT LAST HE MADE HIS WAY, THROUGH ZURICH AND PARIS, TO LONDON.
LONDON
PARIS
ZURICH
HE ARRIVED IN THE EARLY MORNING AND TOOK A CAB TO THE HOUSE OCCUPIED BY NIKOLAI LENIN.
THERE HE MET FOR THE FIRST TIME THE MAN WITH WHOM HE WAS TO HAVE A WARY AND CONTENTIOUS FRIENDSHIP FOR THE NEXT 22 YEARS.
OUR PERO HAS ARRIVED!

THAT MORNING THE TWO MEN TOOK A STROLL ABOUT LONDON.

FROM A BRIDGE LENIN POINTED OUT THE FAMOUS LANDMARKS OF THE CITY.

THE OLDER MAN QUIZZED THE YOUNGER ON HIS REVOLUTIONARY IDEALS, HIS PROGRESS IN THE EAST, AND HIS THEORIES FOR SOCIALIST ACTION.

THE NEW PRODIGY WAS INTRODUCED TO THE OTHER MEMBERS OF THE *ISKRA* BOARD.

MARTOV

AXELROD

ZASULICH

POTRESOV

PLEKHANOV

AMONG THEM, THEY COVERED MANY SHADES OF SOCIALIST OPINION, A REFLECTION OF THE FRAGMENTARY NATURE OF THE MOVEMENT AT THAT TIME.

TROTSKY WAS IMMEDIATELY PUT TO WORK, WRITING ANNOUNCEMENTS, NOTICES, AND SHORT PIECES...

...BUT MOVING QUICKLY TO MAJOR ARTICLES AND EDITORIALS.

PROPAGANDA—THE MARSHALING OF IMAGERY, THE CREATION OF SLOGANS—WAS SEEN AS CRUCIAL TO THE REVOLUTION.

HE GAVE HIS FIRST PUBLIC LECTURE BEFORE A CROWD IN THE WHITECHAPEL DISTRICT OF LONDON.

FINDING HE HAD A CERTAIN SKILL AT IT, THE ORGANIZATION SENT HIM ON A LECTURE TOUR OF BRUSSELS, LIÈGE, AND PARIS.

IN THE FRENCH CAPITAL, HE MET THE YOUNG ACTIVIST NATALIA SEDOVA, AGE 21, WHO HAD BEEN RECRUITED TO GUIDE HIM ABOUT THE CITY.

WITH HER, HE TOURED THE GREAT ARTISTIC HERITAGE OF WESTERN CIVILIZATION, WHICH HE ENDEAVORED TO APPRECIATE.

BEFORE THE END OF 1903 THEY WERE MARRIED AND LIVING IN GENEVA, SWITZERLAND, WHERE *ISKRA* HAD TRANSFERRED ITS EDITORIAL OFFICES.

BY THIS TIME TROTSKY'S MARRIAGE TO ALEXANDRA HAD BEEN DISSOLVED. SHE HAD MADE HER WAY OUT OF SIBERIA WITH THEIR DAUGHTERS AND ALSO TOOK UP RESIDENCE BRIEFLY IN GENEVA BEFORE RETURNING TO RUSSIA.

SHE AND HER EX-HUSBAND REMAINED FRIENDS AND COMRADES.

THE SECOND CONGRESS OF THE RUSSIAN SOCIAL DEMOCRATIC LABOR PARTY (RSDLP) MET IN LONDON AND BRUSSELS, JULY 30–AUGUST 23, 1903.

IT WAS TO BE A DIVISIVE MEETING, WITH UNTOLD CONSEQUENCES FOR THE PARTY AND ITS CAUSE.

TO ENSURE THE SUCCESS OF THE REVOLUTION, HOW SHOULD THE PARTY ORGANIZE ITSELF? IT WAS A PROFOUND QUESTION AT THIS TIME.

LENIN ARGUED FOR AN IDEOLOGICALLY PURE BRAND OF MARXISM, A PARTY MADE UP OF DEDICATED PROFESSIONAL REVOLUTIONARIES AND CONTROLLED BY A STRONG CENTRAL COMMITTEE WITH A RIGID HIERARCHY. THE USE OF TERRORISM WOULD NOT BE RENOUNCED.

THE CONTRARY VIEW, LED BY YURI MARTOV, ADVOCATED A LOOSER PARTY STRUCTURE, DECENTRALIZED AND HOME TO MANY SHADES OF LEFTIST OPINION. IT WOULD REACH OUT TO THE MIDDLE CLASS AND CONVENTIONAL LIBERALS WITHIN THE EXISTING ORDER—THE BOURGEOISIE SO LOATHED BY LENIN.

TROTSKY, STILL HOLDING TO THE IDEAL OF SMALL, SEMIAUTONOMOUS CELLS, FOUND HIMSELF GENERALLY IN SUPPORT OF THIS GROUP.

BY THE END OF THE CONGRESS THE PARTY HAD SPLIT INTO TWO OPPOSING FACTIONS: LENIN'S BOLSHEVIKS (MAJORITY)...

...AND MARTOV'S MENSHEVIKS (MINORITY).

23

FROM THIS POINT TROTSKY, THOUGH NOMINALLY A MENSHEVIK, ATTEMPTED TO STEER A MIDDLE COURSE BETWEEN THE TWO FACTIONS. HE PREFERRED A SINGLE UNITED PARTY.

IN SEPTEMBER 1904 HE SOUGHT TO SEPARATE HIMSELF FROM RUSSIAN ÉMIGRÉ CIRCLES, AND MOVED BRIEFLY TO MUNICH. GERMANY WAS AT THAT TIME CONSIDERED THE NATION MOST RIPE FOR REVOLUTION.

THERE HE LIVED IN THE HOME OF A. L. HELPHAND, KNOWN AS PARVUS, A VETERAN WRITER FOR *ISKRA* AND OTHER PUBLICATIONS.

THE OLDER MAN SHARED WITH TROTSKY A DISTRUST OF LENIN'S IDEAS OF CENTRAL AUTHORITY, AND THE TWO OF THEM FORMED A BRIEF ALLIANCE.

THE SPLIT IN THE PARTY LED TO A SPLIT IN THE RANKS OF THE *ISKRA* BOARD.

GRADUALLY TROTSKY SEVERED ALL CONNECTION TO THE PUBLICATION.

TO HIM, LENIN'S METHODS WOULD LEAD...

...TO THE PARTY ORGANIZATION SUBSTITUTING ITSELF FOR THE PARTY, THE CENTRAL COMMITTEE SUBSTITUTING ITSELF FOR THE PARTY ORGANIZATION, AND FINALLY THE DICTATOR SUBSTITUTING HIMSELF FOR THE CENTRAL COMMITTEE.

BY THIS TIME A WAR BETWEEN RUSSIA AND JAPAN HAD BEEN DRAGGING ON FOR SEVERAL MONTHS.

THE TSARIST GOVERNMENT, SEEKING TO EXPAND ITS HOLDINGS IN THE FAR EAST, WAS CHALLENGED BY THE SIMILARLY INCLINED EMPIRE OF JAPAN.

TROTSKY WAS DISGUSTED TO SEE MANY MENSHEVIKS AND OTHER SOCIALISTS RALLY PATRIOTICALLY BEHIND THE NATIONAL CAUSE.

BUT AS RUSSIA HEADED TOWARD A HUMILIATING DEFEAT, PUBLIC DISSATISFACTION WITH THE REGIME GREW DRAMATICALLY.

ALL LEVELS OF RUSSIAN SOCIETY WERE DEMANDING MORE DIRECT PARTICIPATION IN THEIR GOVERNMENT. THE TIME SEEMED RIPE FOR FUNDAMENTAL CHANGE.

A PLAN WAS PUT FORWARD TO PETITION THE TSAR TO GRANT AN ELECTED NATIONAL ASSEMBLY.

MENSHEVIK LEADERS WERE OPTIMISTIC THAT ANTITSARIST ALLIANCES COULD BE FORMED WITH LIBERALS AND OTHER MODERATE ELEMENTS.

TROTSKY OBJECTED TO THIS APPROACH AND EVENTUALLY BROKE COMPLETELY WITH THE MENSHEVIK FACTION.

HE ENVISIONED A REVOLUTION FROM THE BOTTOM UP. THE WORKING CLASS, ACTING INDEPENDENTLY, WAS THE KEY TO A NEW SOCIAL AND ECONOMIC ORDER.

IT WAS TIME, HE KNEW, FOR THE EXILED REVOLUTIONARIES TO RETURN TO THEIR HOMELAND.

THE OPPORTUNITY SUDDENLY AROSE WHEN HE SAW A SHOCKING REPORT IN THE GENEVA NEWSPAPER.

AFTER HE READ IT, "A DULL, BURNING SENSATION SEEMED TO OVERPOWER ME."

PART ☭ THREE

THE YEAR 1905

ST. PETERSBURG, JANUARY 22, 1905. A GREAT MASS OF UNARMED MEN, WOMEN, AND CHILDREN, LED BY AN ORTHODOX PRIEST, FATHER GAPON, MARCHED ON THE WINTER PALACE TO SUBMIT A PETITION OF GRIEVANCES.

КОНТРОЛЬ РАБОЧИХ НАД ПРОИЗВОД

THEY WERE MET BY MOUNTED GOVERNMENT TROOPS, WHO MERCILESSLY SHOT THEM DOWN IN WHAT BECAME KNOWN AS THE BLOODY SUNDAY MASSACRE.

MORE THAN 1,000 WERE KILLED OR WOUNDED.

DECIDING THAT HE COULD STAY ABROAD NO LONGER, LEON TROTSKY AND HIS WIFE LEFT AT ONCE FOR RUSSIA.

ON FORGED PASSPORTS, THEY TRAVELED FROM GENEVA TO MUNICH AND FROM THERE TO VIENNA.

IN FEBRUARY THEY ARRIVED IN KIEV, WHERE THEY REMAINED FOR SEVERAL MONTHS, LIVING IN A SERIES OF SAFE HOUSES.

THERE, A GROUP OF BOLSHEVIKS MAINTAINED AN UNDERGROUND PRINTING PRESS, WHICH THEY HAD KEPT IN OPERATION FOR SEVERAL YEARS, UNDER THE NOSES OF THE SECRET POLICE.

WHILE IN KIEV, TROTSKY KEPT HIMSELF BUSY WRITING PROCLAMATIONS, DECLARATIONS, AND BROADSIDES.

BY SPRING, THROUGH BOLSHEVIK CONNECTIONS, HE AND NATALIA FOUND THEIR WAY TO ST. PETERSBURG.

TROTSKY REMAINED IN CONTACT WITH BOTH THE BOLSHEVIK AND MENSHEVIK GROUPS AS EVENTS QUICKLY OUTPACED THEIR ABILITY TO CONTROL THEM.

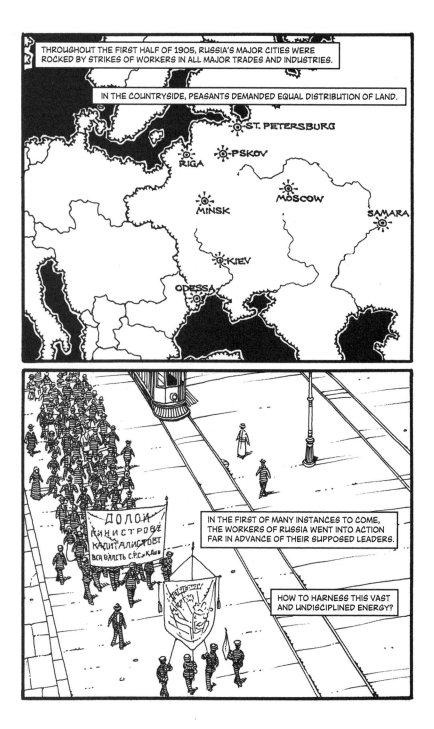

THROUGHOUT THE FIRST HALF OF 1905, RUSSIA'S MAJOR CITIES WERE ROCKED BY STRIKES OF WORKERS IN ALL MAJOR TRADES AND INDUSTRIES.

IN THE COUNTRYSIDE, PEASANTS DEMANDED EQUAL DISTRIBUTION OF LAND.

ST. PETERSBURG

PSKOV

RIGA

MOSCOW

MINSK

SAMARA

KIEV

ODESSA

IN THE FIRST OF MANY INSTANCES TO COME, THE WORKERS OF RUSSIA WENT INTO ACTION FAR IN ADVANCE OF THEIR SUPPOSED LEADERS.

HOW TO HARNESS THIS VAST AND UNDISCIPLINED ENERGY?

ONCE IN ST. PETERSBURG, TROTSKY WENT TO WORK PRODUCING A HUGE NUMBER OF ARTICLES FOR SEVERAL NEWSPAPERS AND BROADSHEETS.

HE PROPHESIED THAT ONCE THE WORKERS OF THE URBAN AREAS ROSE UP, THE PEASANTRY WOULD FOLLOW THEIR LEAD. THEN THE DOOR WOULD BE OPEN FOR THE SOCIAL DEMOCRATS TO TAKE THE REVOLUTION TO COMPLETION, TO GIVE IT STRUCTURE AND PURPOSE.

ЧТОД

ОКТЯБРЬС

БОТН

HE RECOGNIZED EARLY THAT A PARTICULAR PROBLEM MIGHT LIE WITH THE PEASANTRY, ESPECIALLY THE WEALTHIER OF THEM— LIKE HIS OWN FATHER!

FIERCELY INDEPENDENT AND NATURALLY CONSERVATIVE, THEY REPRESENTED A SPECIAL PROPAGANDISTIC CHALLENGE.

THE MILITARY WAS A RIPE VENUE FOR RADICAL CONVERSION, AS THE CASUALTIES MOUNTED IN THE ONGOING AND DISASTROUS WAR WITH JAPAN.

THE WAR WOULD END IN SEPTEMBER 1905, WITH RUSSIA GIVING UP MUCH OF ITS PACIFIC TERRITORY.

ON MAY 1 NATALIA WAS ARRESTED, ALONG WITH SEVERAL OTHERS, WHILE ATTEMPTING TO ORGANIZE A SECRET POLITICAL MEETING.

HER HUSBAND WAS ADVISED TO HIDE OUT FOR A WHILE.

HE FLED TO FINLAND, TAKING UP RESIDENCE IN AN ISOLATED TOWN.

HE WROTE FURIOUSLY AND TOOK TRANQUIL WALKS IN THE COUNTRYSIDE.

IN SEPTEMBER, HE MOVED TO AN EVEN MORE REMOTE LOCATION...

...ALL THE WHILE KEEPING UP WITH EVENTS AT HOME VIA NEWSPAPER.

ONE DAY IN EARLY OCTOBER HE READ OF DRAMATIC DEVELOPMENTS IN RUSSIA: THE REVOLUTION...IN FULL SWING.

BY THAT EVENING HE WAS BACK IN ST. PETERSBURG.

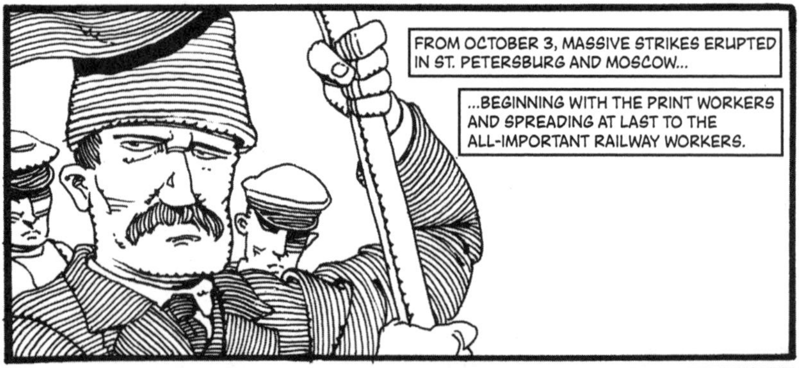
FROM OCTOBER 3, MASSIVE STRIKES ERUPTED IN ST. PETERSBURG AND MOSCOW...
...BEGINNING WITH THE PRINT WORKERS AND SPREADING AT LAST TO THE ALL-IMPORTANT RAILWAY WORKERS.

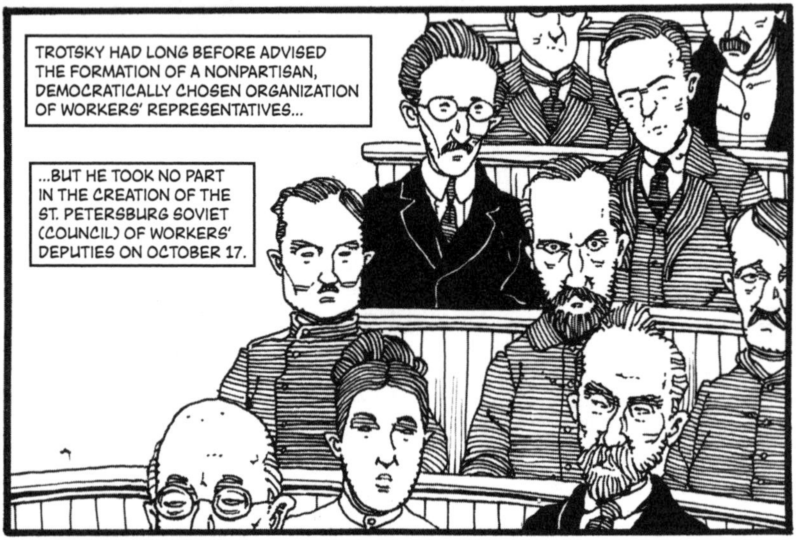
TROTSKY HAD LONG BEFORE ADVISED THE FORMATION OF A NONPARTISAN, DEMOCRATICALLY CHOSEN ORGANIZATION OF WORKERS' REPRESENTATIVES...
...BUT HE TOOK NO PART IN THE CREATION OF THE ST. PETERSBURG SOVIET (COUNCIL) OF WORKERS' DEPUTIES ON OCTOBER 17.

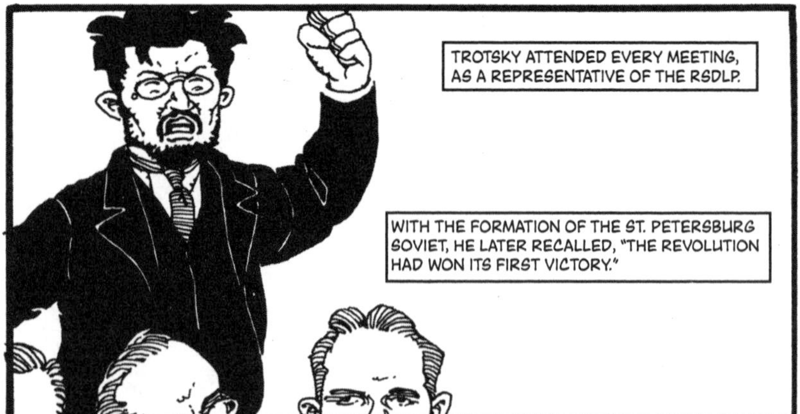
TROTSKY ATTENDED EVERY MEETING, AS A REPRESENTATIVE OF THE RSDLP.
WITH THE FORMATION OF THE ST. PETERSBURG SOVIET, HE LATER RECALLED, "THE REVOLUTION HAD WON ITS FIRST VICTORY."

LATER IN THE MONTH, IN THE FACE OF A NATIONWIDE STRIKE, THE TSAR AT LAST RELENTED.

HE ISSUED A PROCLAMATION AUTHORIZING THE CREATION OF A LEGISLATIVE ASSEMBLY (DUMA) FOR THE FIRST TIME IN RUSSIAN HISTORY.

A FURTHER DECREE ORDERED THE RELEASE OF MOST POLITICAL PRISONERS.

TROTSKY AND NATALIA WERE REUNITED.

FOR THE REVOLUTIONARIES, THIS WAS AN INCOMPLETE VICTORY, BUT TROTSKY URGED RETRENCHMENT AND STOCKTAKING.

EVENTS ARE WORKING FOR US, AND THERE IS NO ADVANTAGE FOR US IN FORCING THEIR PROGRESS... FOR TOMORROW WE SHALL BE STRONGER THAN WE ARE TODAY.

FURTHER STRIKES WERE CALLED OFF AS REVOLUTIONARY FERVOR DISSIPATED THROUGHOUT THE COUNTRY.

SLOWLY WORKERS RETURNED TO THE FACTORIES.

TROTSKY CONTINUED HIS WORK WITH THE ST. PETERSBURG SOVIET.

UNDER HIS GUIDANCE, THE BODY ISSUED A "FINANCIAL MANIFESTO" PREDICTING THE INEVITABLE BANKRUPTCY OF THE ROMANOV DYNASTY.

ON THE EVENING OF DECEMBER 3, GOVERNMENT TROOPS, WHICH HAD REMAINED LOYAL TO THE TSAR, SURROUNDED THE MEETING HALL OF THE SOVIET.

NO RESISTANCE TO BE MADE! NO ARMS TO BE SURRENDERED!

THE HALL WAS OVERRUN. TROTSKY AND THE OTHER LEADERS OF THE SOVIET WERE PLACED UNDER ARREST.

PART FOUR

PRISON AND EXILE AGAIN

TROTSKY'S SECOND STAY IN PRISON PROVED FAR EASIER THAN HIS FIRST. THE ELECTION OF THE FIRST DUMA IN APRIL 1906 BROUGHT WITH IT A NEW STIMULATION OF POLITICAL REFORM.

KRESTY PRISON

PETER-PAUL FORTRESS

HOUSE OF PRELIMINARY DETENTION

HE JOKED THAT NOW HE COULD READ AND WRITE AS HE PLEASED AND NOT WORRY ABOUT GOING TO PRISON.

ON SEPTEMBER 19, 1906, THE LEADERS OF THE ST. PETERSBURG SOVIET WERE PUT ON TRIAL.

TROTSKY'S AGED PARENTS WERE IN ATTENDANCE.

AT ONE POINT, WHILE BEING QUESTIONED, TROTSKY SUFFERED ONE OF HIS FAINTING SPELLS.

THE DEFENDANTS WERE NOT ALLOWED TO CALL THE WITNESSES THEY DESIRED, SO IN THE END THEY ELECTED TO BOYCOTT THE PROCEEDINGS.

THE VERDICT WAS READ TO AN EMPTY COURTROOM. THE SENTENCE: ENFORCED SETTLEMENT EXILE FOR AN INDEFINITE PERIOD AND LOSS OF ALL CIVIL RIGHTS.

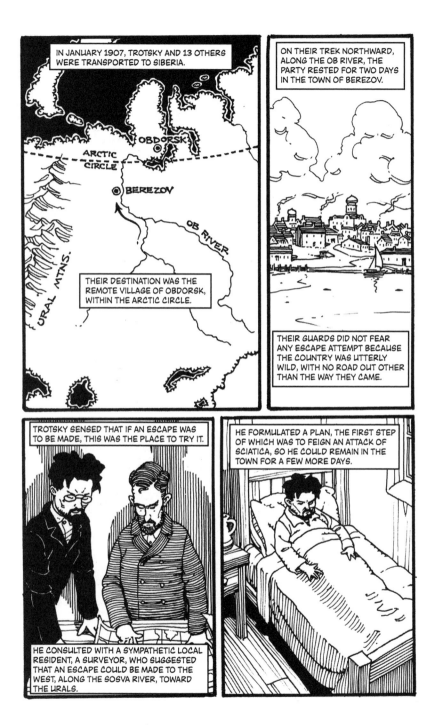

IN JANUARY 1907, TROTSKY AND 13 OTHERS WERE TRANSPORTED TO SIBERIA.

OBDORSK

ARCTIC CIRCLE

BEREZOV

OB RIVER

URAL MTNS.

THEIR DESTINATION WAS THE REMOTE VILLAGE OF OBDORSK, WITHIN THE ARCTIC CIRCLE.

ON THEIR TREK NORTHWARD, ALONG THE OB RIVER, THE PARTY RESTED FOR TWO DAYS IN THE TOWN OF BEREZOV.

THEIR GUARDS DID NOT FEAR ANY ESCAPE ATTEMPT BECAUSE THE COUNTRY WAS UTTERLY WILD, WITH NO ROAD OUT OTHER THAN THE WAY THEY CAME.

TROTSKY SENSED THAT IF AN ESCAPE WAS TO BE MADE, THIS WAS THE PLACE TO TRY IT.

HE CONSULTED WITH A SYMPATHETIC LOCAL RESIDENT, A SURVEYOR, WHO SUGGESTED THAT AN ESCAPE COULD BE MADE TO THE WEST, ALONG THE SOSVA RIVER, TOWARD THE URALS.

HE FORMULATED A PLAN, THE FIRST STEP OF WHICH WAS TO FEIGN AN ATTACK OF SCIATICA, SO HE COULD REMAIN IN THE TOWN FOR A FEW MORE DAYS.

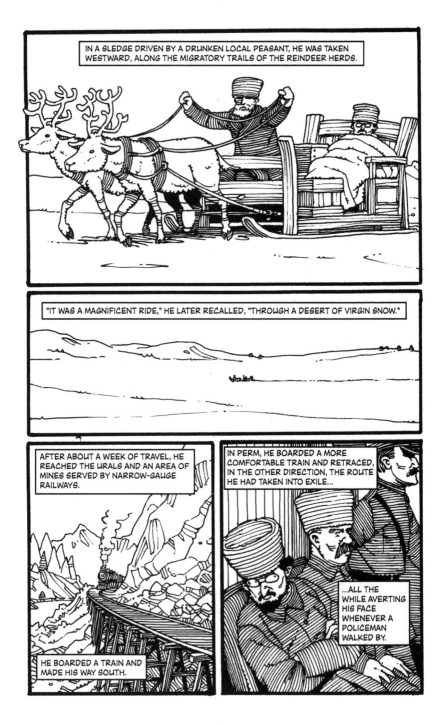

IN A SLEDGE DRIVEN BY A DRUNKEN LOCAL PEASANT, HE WAS TAKEN WESTWARD, ALONG THE MIGRATORY TRAILS OF THE REINDEER HERDS.

"IT WAS A MAGNIFICENT RIDE," HE LATER RECALLED, "THROUGH A DESERT OF VIRGIN SNOW."

AFTER ABOUT A WEEK OF TRAVEL, HE REACHED THE URALS AND AN AREA OF MINES SERVED BY NARROW-GAUGE RAILWAYS.

HE BOARDED A TRAIN AND MADE HIS WAY SOUTH.

IN PERM, HE BOARDED A MORE COMFORTABLE TRAIN AND RETRACED, IN THE OTHER DIRECTION, THE ROUTE HE HAD TAKEN INTO EXILE...

...ALL THE WHILE AVERTING HIS FACE WHENEVER A POLICEMAN WALKED BY.

IN ST. PETERSBURG HE WAS JOINED BY NATALIA...

SWEDEN

FINLAND

HELSINKI

ST. PETERSBURG

...AND TOGETHER THEY SLIPPED INTO FINLAND, THERE TO BEGIN ANOTHER LONG PERIOD OF FOREIGN EXILE.

IN THAT COUNTRY HE WAS REUNITED WITH LENIN, WHO HAD FLED THERE AFTER THE EVENTS OF 1905.

HAVING TAKEN NO ACTIVE PART IN THE ST. PETERSBURG SOVIET, THE OLDER LEADER HAD MANAGED TO AVOID ARREST.

THE FIFTH CONGRESS OF THE RSDLP WAS HELD IN MAY 1907 AT A SOCIALIST CHURCH IN LONDON.

TROTSKY REMEMBERED IT AS "A PROTRACTED, CROWDED, STORMY AND CHAOTIC" MEETING.

HE ENTERED THE CONGRESS WITH A GREAT DEGREE OF OPTIMISM: THE YEAR 1905 HAD BEEN BUT A DRESS REHEARSAL; TIME WAS ON THEIR SIDE.

WHAT HE FOUND WAS A PARTY TORN APART IN SEVERAL DIFFERENT DIRECTIONS, OVER MANY DIFFERENT ISSUES.

AMONG THE QUESTIONS IN THE AIR: WHAT WOULD A POSTREVOLUTIONARY RUSSIA LOOK LIKE?

HOW CLOSELY SHOULD THE SOCIAL DEMOCRATS ALLY THEMSELVES WITH THE LIBERAL ELEMENTS WITHIN THE DUMA?

WHAT POLICY SHOULD BE ADOPTED TOWARD THE PEASANTRY?

OVER IT ALL WAS THE OLD PROBLEM OF PARTY STRUCTURE. HOW IDEOLOGICALLY UNIFIED SHOULD THEY BE?

LENIN THOUGHT THAT THE RANKS SHOULD BE CLEANSED OF ANY "DEVIATIONISTS" AND "FACTIONALISTS."

TROTSKY, KEEPING A DISTANCE FROM THE COMPETING GROUPS, ATTEMPTED TO ACT AS A MEDIATOR AND CONCILIATOR. TO HIM, A HEALTHY PARTY OFFERED A UNITY IN DIVERSITY.

FOR HIS TROUBLE, HIS POSITION WAS BRANDED AS JUST ANOTHER FACTION. LENIN CALLED HIM A JUDAS.

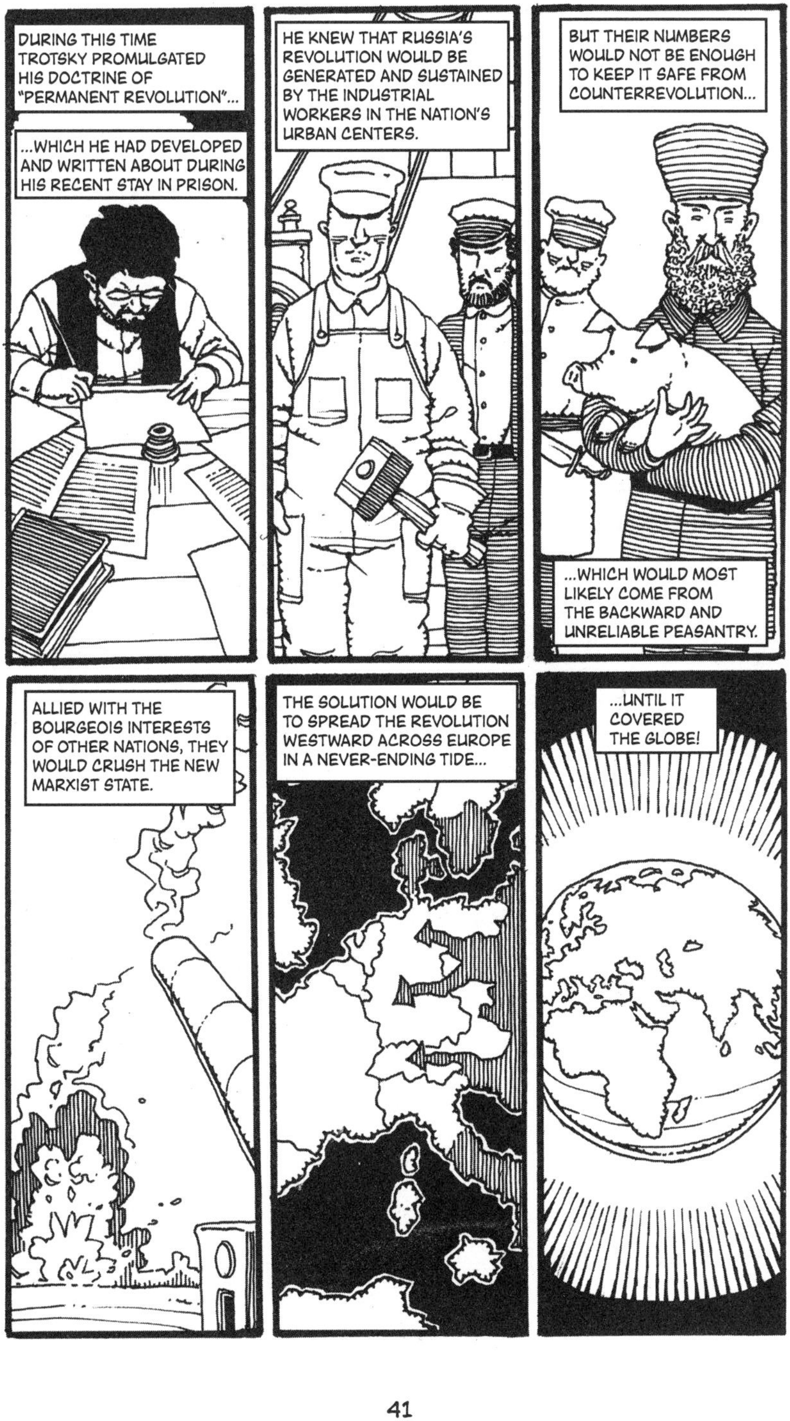
DURING THIS TIME TROTSKY PROMULGATED HIS DOCTRINE OF "PERMANENT REVOLUTION"...
...WHICH HE HAD DEVELOPED AND WRITTEN ABOUT DURING HIS RECENT STAY IN PRISON.
HE KNEW THAT RUSSIA'S REVOLUTION WOULD BE GENERATED AND SUSTAINED BY THE INDUSTRIAL WORKERS IN THE NATION'S URBAN CENTERS.
BUT THEIR NUMBERS WOULD NOT BE ENOUGH TO KEEP IT SAFE FROM COUNTERREVOLUTION...
...WHICH WOULD MOST LIKELY COME FROM THE BACKWARD AND UNRELIABLE PEASANTRY.
ALLIED WITH THE BOURGEOIS INTERESTS OF OTHER NATIONS, THEY WOULD CRUSH THE NEW MARXIST STATE.
THE SOLUTION WOULD BE TO SPREAD THE REVOLUTION WESTWARD ACROSS EUROPE IN A NEVER-ENDING TIDE...
...UNTIL IT COVERED THE GLOBE!

IN OCTOBER 1907, TROTSKY AND HIS FAMILY SETTLED IN VIENNA...

...WHERE A COMMUNITY OF RUSSIAN EXILES WAS ESTABLISHED.

THERE HE ATTEMPTED TO SUSTAIN A LIVING AS CONTRIBUTOR TO SEVERAL PUBLICATIONS...

...CHIEF AMONG THEM THE REGIONAL JOURNAL *KIEVAN THOUGHT*.

BY THIS TIME HE AND NATALIA HAD TWO YOUNG SONS...

...LEV (BORN 1906) AND SERGEI (BORN 1908).

IN OCTOBER 1908 HE STARTED HIS OWN RUSSIAN-LANGUAGE PERIODICAL, *PRAVDA* (TRUTH).

ПРАВДА

ITS MISSION: TO REUNITE THE SOCIAL DEMOCRATS!

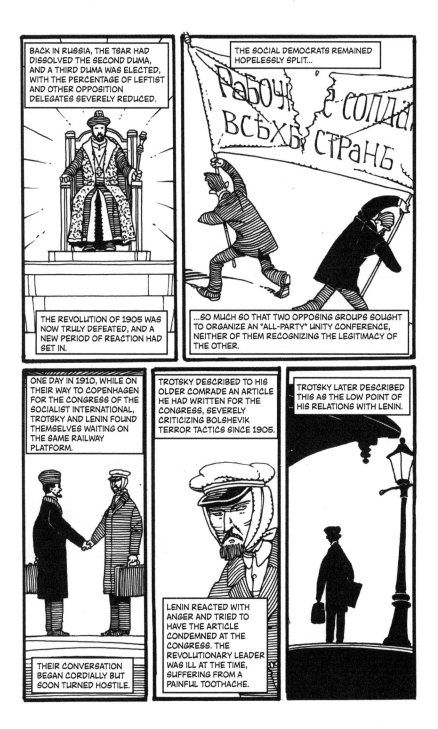

BACK IN RUSSIA, THE TSAR HAD DISSOLVED THE SECOND DUMA, AND A THIRD DUMA WAS ELECTED, WITH THE PERCENTAGE OF LEFTIST AND OTHER OPPOSITION DELEGATES SEVERELY REDUCED.

THE REVOLUTION OF 1905 WAS NOW TRULY DEFEATED, AND A NEW PERIOD OF REACTION HAD SET IN.

THE SOCIAL DEMOCRATS REMAINED HOPELESSLY SPLIT...

...SO MUCH SO THAT TWO OPPOSING GROUPS SOUGHT TO ORGANIZE AN "ALL-PARTY" UNITY CONFERENCE, NEITHER OF THEM RECOGNIZING THE LEGITIMACY OF THE OTHER.

ONE DAY IN 1910, WHILE ON THEIR WAY TO COPENHAGEN FOR THE CONGRESS OF THE SOCIALIST INTERNATIONAL, TROTSKY AND LENIN FOUND THEMSELVES WAITING ON THE SAME RAILWAY PLATFORM.

THEIR CONVERSATION BEGAN CORDIALLY BUT SOON TURNED HOSTILE.

TROTSKY DESCRIBED TO HIS OLDER COMRADE AN ARTICLE HE HAD WRITTEN FOR THE CONGRESS, SEVERELY CRITICIZING BOLSHEVIK TERROR TACTICS SINCE 1905.

LENIN REACTED WITH ANGER AND TRIED TO HAVE THE ARTICLE CONDEMNED AT THE CONGRESS. THE REVOLUTIONARY LEADER WAS ILL AT THE TIME, SUFFERING FROM A PAINFUL TOOTHACHE.

TROTSKY LATER DESCRIBED THIS AS THE LOW POINT OF HIS RELATIONS WITH LENIN.

43

TROTSKY BECAME DISILLUSIONED WITH THE RANCOR AND DIVISIVENESS OF SOCIALIST POLITICS AND IN THE AUTUMN OF 1912 DISCONTINUED *PRAVDA*. (THE BOLSHEVIKS HAD BY THEN ESTABLISHED THEMSELVES AS A SEPARATE PARTY AND APPROPRIATED THE TITLE FOR THEIR OWN NEWSPAPER.)

HE WAS SENT BY *KIEVAN THOUGHT* TO THE VOLATILE BALKAN REGION, WHOSE GROUPING OF JEALOUS LITTLE STATES HAD JUST EXPLODED INTO WAR.

USING HIS OLD PEN NAME ANTID OTO, HE DESCRIBED SOLDIERS MARCHING FROM BELGRADE, EACH WEARING SANDALS AND A JAUNTY SPRIG OF GREEN IN HIS CAP.

THEY HAD "THE LOOK OF MEN DOOMED FOR SACRIFICE."

HE RESERVED HIS GREATEST ANGER FOR EACH NATION'S "SCIENTIFICALLY ORGANIZED SYSTEM OF DUPING PUBLIC OPINION."

HE LATER RECALLED THAT "A SENSE OF THE TRAGEDY OF HISTORY WAS TAKING POSSESSION OF ME; A FEELING OF IMPOTENCE BEFORE FATE, A BURNING COMPASSION FOR THE HUMAN LOCUST."

44

ON JUNE 28, 1914, ARCHDUKE FRANZ FERDINAND WAS ASSASSINATED IN SARAJEVO, IN THE AUSTRIAN PROVINCE OF BOSNIA, BY A SERB NATIONALIST.

WHAT COULD HAVE BEEN SEEN AS JUST ANOTHER OUTRAGE IN THE ONGOING BALKAN CONFLICT BECAME THE SPARK FOR AN UNPRECEDENTED WORLD WAR.

WITHIN DAYS AUSTRIA-HUNGARY DECLARED WAR ON SERBIA, GERMANY DECLARED WAR ON RUSSIA AND FRANCE, GREAT BRITAIN DECLARED WAR ON GERMANY...

ВОЙНА

...AND SO ON UNTIL THE ENTIRE CONTINENT WAS IMMERSED IN CONFLICT.

RUSSIA BEGAN MOBILIZING ITS RESOURCES TO GREAT PUBLIC SUPPORT.

TROTSKY WAS ONCE AGAIN DISMAYED TO SEE HOW THE SOCIALIST PARTIES IN ALL COUNTRIES RALLIED TO SUPPORT THEIR NATIONAL CRUSADE. EVEN IN GERMANY, THE SOCIAL DEMOCRATIC PARTY VOTED TO ENDORSE THE WAR.

SUCH, HE DECLARED, WERE "TRAITORS TO THE CAUSE."

AS THE WORKING CLASS OF VIENNA MASSED IN THE STREETS IN SUPPORT OF THEIR GOVERNMENT, TROTSKY KNEW IT WAS TIME TO LEAVE.

HE AND HIS FAMILY AT ONCE DEPARTED FOR SWITZERLAND.

45

LEAVING HIS WIFE AND SONS IN ZURICH, HE RELOCATED TO PARIS...

...THERE TO CONTINUE HIS WORK AS WAR CORRESPONDENT FOR *KIEVAN THOUGHT.*

TO HIM, MARXISM, AS A TRULY INTERNATIONAL MOVEMENT, MUST LEAD A "STRUGGLE FOR PEACE"...

...AND PEACE COULD COME ONLY WHEN THE WORKING CLASSES OF ALL NATIONS DEPOSE THE CAPITALIST INTERESTS THAT ARE BEHIND ALL WARS.

TO THIS END HE EDITED AND PUBLISHED A SHORT-LIVED NEWSPAPER, *STRUGGLE.*

FURTHER, HE BELIEVED, THE WAR MIGHT JUST PROVIDE A FERTILE GROUND FOR THE GROWING REVOLUTION.

IN SEVERAL WAYS THE MASS DEPLOYMENTS AND PLANNED ECONOMIES OF THE WARTIME STATE WOULD PRECONDITION THE PROLETARIAT TO ORGANIZED REVOLT.

LENIN WENT EVEN FURTHER: IT WAS THE DUTY OF EVERY SOCIALIST TO WORK FOR RUSSIA'S DEFEAT IN THE WORLD WAR. A VICTORY BY THE TSARIST GOVERNMENT WOULD BE UNTHINKABLE.

ПРАВДА

FOR THIS, THE BOLSHEVIKS WERE ACCUSED OF BEING IN LEAGUE WITH THE GERMAN EMPIRE.

IN MAY 1915, TROTSKY BROUGHT HIS FAMILY TO PARIS.

IN A SHORT TIME HE WAS AN EDITOR FOR THE RUSSIAN ÉMIGRÉ NEWSPAPER *NASHE SLOVO* (OUR WORD).

HE REPRESENTED THE PUBLICATION AT THE 1915 CONFERENCE OF ANTIWAR SOCIALISTS IN ZIMMERWALD, SWITZERLAND.

THE RIFT BETWEEN HIM AND LENIN REMAINED AS WIDE AS EVER.

THE TROTSKYS WERE NOT TO REMAIN IN FRANCE FOR LONG.

PRESUMABLY, COPIES OF *NASHE SLOVO* WERE FOUND IN THE POSSESSION OF MUTINOUS RUSSIAN SAILORS IN THE FRENCH PORT OF TOULON.

IN SEPTEMBER 1916, TROTSKY WAS ESCORTED FROM HIS APARTMENT BY THE FRENCH POLICE...

...AND DEPORTED TO SPAIN.

BUT THE SPANISH DID NOT WANT HIM EITHER, AND HIS FATE REMAINED IN FLUX FOR SEVERAL MONTHS.

IN RUSSIA, AS 1916 DREW TO A CLOSE, PUBLIC SUPPORT FOR THE TSAR AND HIS WAR POLICIES REACHED AN ALL-TIME LOW.

FOOD AND FUEL SHORTAGES SPREAD NATIONWIDE.

A FOCUS OF PARTICULAR OUTRAGE WAS THE DEBAUCHED RELIGIOUS MYSTIC RASPUTIN, WHO HELD A MYSTERIOUS INFLUENCE OVER THE ROYAL FAMILY.

IN DECEMBER THE "MAD MONK" WAS ASSASSINATED BY COUSINS OF THE TSAR.

LATER THAT MONTH 37-YEAR-OLD LEON TROTSKY LEFT SPAIN FOR AMERICA...

...AS THE DECISIVE YEAR OF 1917 LOOMED OVER THE HORIZON.

PART FIVE

THE YEAR 1917

ON SUNDAY, JANUARY 13, 1917, TROTSKY AND HIS FAMILY ARRIVED IN NEW YORK HARBOR. HE LATER CONFESSED TO MIXED FEELINGS ABOUT THIS CENTER OF WORLD CAPITALISM...

...RECALLING, "COLD. WIND. RAIN. ON LAND, A WET MOUNTAIN OF BUILDINGS. THE NEW WORLD!"

FROM THE MOMENT OF HIS ARRIVAL, HIS EVERY MOVEMENT WAS RECORDED BY THE PRESS...

...AND SCRUTINIZED BY THE AMERICAN SECRET SERVICE.

THE FAMILY FOUND AN APARTMENT IN THE BOROUGH OF THE BRONX...

...AND FURNISHED IT ON THE INSTALLMENT PLAN.

LEV AND SERGEI WERE ESPECIALLY AMAZED BY THE ARRAY OF LUXURIES AVAILABLE TO THEM...

...ELECTRIC LIGHTS, A GAS COOKING RANGE, A BATH IN EVERY APARTMENT, AUTOMATIC ELEVATORS, AND MOST OF ALL THE TELEPHONE.

TROTSKY BEGAN TO CONTRIBUTE ARTICLES AND EDITORIALS TO NEW YORK'S RUSSIAN-LANGUAGE NEWSPAPER NOVY MIR (NEW WORLD).

HE ALSO GAVE LECTURES IN RUSSIAN AND GERMAN TO AUDIENCES IN NEW YORK, PHILADELPHIA, AND OTHER CITIES.

I LEFT A EUROPE WALLOWING IN BLOOD, BUT I LEFT WITH A PROFOUND FAITH IN THE COMING REVOLUTION.

HE FOUND THAT THE IDEAS OF THE AMERICAN SOCIALIST PARTY LAGGED BEHIND EVEN THE MILDEST OF THEIR EUROPEAN COUNTERPARTS...

...AND WERE PARTICULARLY MARGINALIZED NOW THAT AMERICA WAS PREPARING TO ENTER THE WORLD WAR.

LIBER BOND

AS HAD HAPPENED SO OFTEN BEFORE, TROTSKY LEARNED OF MOMENTOUS EVENTS IN RUSSIA WHILE AWAY IN EXILE.

THUS HE RECEIVED WORD OF THE FEBRUARY REVOLUTION IN EARLY MARCH.

A SPONTANEOUS UPRISING OF WORKERS HAD OVERTHROWN THE IMPERIAL GOVERNMENT AND INSTALLED A DEMOCRATIC SOCIALIST REPUBLIC.

THE TSAR HAD ABDICATED, AND HE AND HIS FAMILY HAD BEEN TRANSPORTED TO INTERNAL EXILE. (THEY WOULD BE EXECUTED THE FOLLOWING YEAR.)

LATER IN MARCH, TROTSKY AND HIS FAMILY, ALONG WITH SEVERAL OTHER RUSSIAN EXPATRIATES, ATTEMPTED TO RETURN HOME ABOARD A NORWEGIAN SHIP...

...BUT THEY WERE TAKEN ASHORE IN NOVA SCOTIA, DETAINED, AND INTERROGATED.

THE BRITISH GOVERNMENT HAD SENT WORD THAT THE SHIP CONTAINED DANGEROUS SUBVERSIVES.

TROTSKY AND THE OTHER RUSSIAN MEN SPENT THE NEXT MONTH IN A POW CAMP.

THE NEW RUSSIAN GOVERNMENT EFFECTED HIS RELEASE, AND EARLY IN MAY, TROTSKY AT LAST ARRIVED IN ST. PETERSBURG, WHICH HAD BEEN RENAMED PETROGRAD TO REMOVE ANY TAINT OF THE GERMAN LANGUAGE.

HE WENT IMMEDIATELY TO THE SMOLNY INSTITUTE, A FORMER ACADEMY FOR YOUNG LADIES, NOW THE HEADQUARTERS OF THE SOVIET OF WORKERS' DEPUTIES.

AT ONCE HE WAS SWEPT INTO A VORTEX OF HUMAN EVENTS THAT RESISTED ANY KIND OF IMPOSED CONTROL OR GUIDANCE.

HE KNEW THAT THE MODERATE PROVISIONAL GOVERNMENT COULD NOT LAST.

NOT ONLY DID ITS LEADERS SUPPORT THE CONTINUING WAR EFFORT...

...BUT THEY ENDORSED FULL RIGHTS FOR THE LAND AND FACTORY OWNERS AND OTHER MEMBERS OF THE CAPITALIST CLASS.

TROTSKY ENTERED THE SOVIET AS REPRESENTATIVE OF A GROUP OF SOCIAL DEMOCRATIC INTERNATIONALISTS KNOWN AS THE INTER-DISTRICTERS.

THIS GROUP WAS IN THE PROCESS OF JOINING FORCES WITH THE BOLSHEVIKS, THOUGH THE BOLSHEVIKS THEMSELVES WERE DIVIDED. MANY BELIEVED THAT THE REVOLUTION HAD REACHED ITS GOAL IN FEBRUARY.

HERE HE WAS REUNITED WITH LENIN. FOR THE FIRST TIME IN MANY YEARS THE TWO WERE IN TOTAL AGREEMENT: THE PROVISIONAL GOVERNMENT MUST BE OVERTHROWN.

KAMENEV

ZINOVIEV

BUT NOW WAS NOT THE MOMENT. THEY MUST BIDE THEIR TIME.

THEY WERE JOINED BY LENIN'S CLOSE ASSOCIATES LEV KAMENEV AND GRIGORII ZINOVIEV.

THE PETROGRAD SOVIET WAS AT THE TIME UNDER THE LEADERSHIP OF PROWAR MENSHEVIKS.

THEY FAVORED AN ALLIANCE WITH THE LIBERALS IN THE DUMA TO FORM A COALITION GOVERNMENT.

AS A MEMBER OF THE SOVIET, TROTSKY CAST HIS FIRST VOTE AGAINST THE FORMATION OF SUCH AN ALLIANCE.

HE WAS NOW A FULL AND UNAPOLOGETIC MEMBER OF THE BOLSHEVIK PARTY.

FOR TROTSKY, A GOVERNMENT OF THE WORKERS WAS ABSOLUTELY ESSENTIAL.

BY THIS TIME EVERY RUSSIAN CITY HAD SOVIETS OF WORKERS' OR SOLDIERS' OR PEASANTS' DEPUTIES. ALL POWER TO THE SOVIETS!

IN MAY THE FIRST CONGRESS OF SOVIETS OF PEASANTS' DEPUTIES DECLARED: "THE RIGHT OF PRIVATE OWNERSHIP OF LAND IS ABOLISHED FOREVER...

...LAND IS LIKE AIR, IT SHOULD NOT BE BOUGHT OR SOLD."

IN JUNE THE FIRST ALL-RUSSIAN CONGRESS OF SOVIETS ASSEMBLED.

LENIN, WHILE NOT A PARTICULARLY CHARISMATIC PUBLIC SPEAKER, WAS UNIVERSALLY RECOGNIZED AS THE NATURAL LEADER OF THE REVOLUTION...

...WHILE TROTSKY WAS GENERALLY SEEN AS ITS MOST SKILLED AND INSPIRING ORATOR.

FOR TROTSKY, THESE WEEKS WERE A "WHIRL OF MASS MEETINGS."

HE SPOKE AT MEETINGS HELD IN PLANTS, IN SCHOOLS, IN THEATERS, IN STREETS AND SQUARES.

"MY AUDIENCE WAS COMPOSED OF WORKERS, SOLDIERS, HARD-WORKING MOTHERS, STREET URCHINS, THE OPPRESSED UNDERDOGS OF THE CAPITAL," TROTSKY REMEMBERED. "EVERY SQUARE INCH WAS FILLED, EVERY HUMAN BODY COMPRESSED TO ITS LIMIT."

ЛИСТОВЪ! УД ДУМУ!

OFTEN IN THIS CROWD WOULD BE HIS TWO DAUGHTERS, ZINA AND NINA, BOTH OF THEM ACTIVE POLITICALLY.

IN SERVICE TO THE REVOLUTION, HIS ENERGY WAS LIMITLESS.

"EACH TIME IT WOULD SEEM TO ME AS IF I COULD NEVER GET THROUGH A NEW MEETING," HE RECALLED, "BUT SOME HIDDEN RESERVE OF NERVOUS ENERGY WOULD COME TO THE SURFACE."

HE COULD BE AWAKENED AT ANY HOUR AND CALLED TO A GATHERING IN A FAR-FLUNG COMMUNITY.

THE SAILORS AT THE KRONSTADT NAVAL BASE SENT A TUG FOR HIM.

IN THE MEANTIME, THE WORLD WAR CONTINUED UNABATED. AMERICA HAD ENTERED THE FRAY IN APRIL, AND THE ALLIES HAILED RUSSIA'S NEW GOVERNMENT AND ITS DETERMINATION TO CONTINUE THE FIGHT.

BUT RUSSIA'S ARMY, PLAGUED BY EQUIPMENT SHORTAGES, HUNGER, AND LOW MORALE, WAS IN NO CONDITION TO CARRY ON.

JUNE SAW THE PROVISIONAL GOVERNMENT INITIATE A MASSIVE OFFENSIVE ALONG ALL ITS MAJOR WAR FRONTS...

RUSSIA

ANY

RIA-HUNGARY

...IN AN INTENSE BUT FUTILE EFFORT TO REVIVE PATRIOTISM AND REUNITE THE COUNTRY.

ROMANIA

SERBIA

BY JULY IT WAS APPARENT TO ALL THAT THE PLAN HAD FAILED. SOLDIERS BY THE THOUSANDS DESERTED THE FRONT.

THEY WERE JOINED IN THE STREETS BY WORKERS, IN THE SPONTANEOUS UPRISING OF "JULY DAYS."

A DEMONSTRATION ON THE STREETS OF PETROGRAD ON JULY 4 WAS MET WITH GUNFIRE FROM GOVERNMENT TROOPS.

HEADQUARTERS OF THE REVOLUTIONARY PARTIES WERE RAIDED AND *PRAVDA* WAS SHUT DOWN.

THE PROVISIONAL GOVERNMENT DISSOLVED AND THEN REORGANIZED ITSELF, WITH A NEW PRIME MINISTER, ALEXANDER KERENSKY.

TROTSKY AND OTHER BOLSHEVIK LEADERS WERE ARRESTED AND PUT IN PRISON.

LENIN, IN DISGUISE, ESCAPED INTO FINLAND.

DURING THEIR VISITS TO THE PRISON TROTSKY WAS PLEASED TO FIND BOTH HIS SONS INCREASINGLY POLITICALLY CONSCIOUS.

THE ELDER, LEV, EVEN ATTACKED ONE YOUNG SOLDIER WHO HAD REFERRED TO HIS FATHER AND LENIN AS GERMAN SPIES.

TROTSKY WAS RELEASED IN EARLY SEPTEMBER AND QUICKLY ELECTED CHAIRMAN OF THE PETROGRAD SOVIET.

FOR THE NEXT SEVERAL WEEKS, WITH LENIN OUT OF THE COUNTRY, HE WAS THE PUBLIC FACE OF THE REVOLUTION.

AFTER THE FAILURE OF THE OFFENSIVE, KERENSKY HAD APPOINTED A NEW COMMANDER IN CHIEF OF THE ARMED FORCES, GENERAL LAVR KORNILOV.

A DEDICATED FOE OF THE REVOLUTION, KORNILOV WAS NOT SO SECRETLY PLANNING A MILITARY TAKEOVER OF THE GOVERNMENT.

SENSING A SHIFT IN THE POLITICAL WIND, KERENSKY DISMISSED THE GENERAL, WHO RESPONDED BY ORDERING HIS TROOPS TO TAKE PETROGRAD.

THEY WERE STOPPED, HOWEVER, BY WORKERS AND SOLDIERS LOYAL TO THE REVOLUTION, CALLING THEMSELVES THE RED GUARD.

KERENSKY PROPOSED THAT A THIRD PROVISIONAL GOVERNMENT BE FORMED, PRECEDED BY A TEMPORARY ASSEMBLY CALLED A PREPARLIAMENT.

THE BOLSHEVIKS, KNOWING THAT THEY WOULD FORM A LARGE PART OF THIS GOVERNMENT, APPROVED THE IDEA. THIS INCLUDED LENIN'S ASSOCIATES KAMENEV AND ZINOVIEV.

TROTSKY REJECTED THE PREPARLIAMENT, CALLING IT A "COUNTERREVOLUTIONARY CONTRIVANCE"...

...WHILE LENIN, FROM HIS REFUGE IN FINLAND, CALLED FOR AN IMMEDIATE SEIZURE OF POWER BY THE BOLSHEVIKS.

BY OCTOBER ALL THE MAJOR SOVIETS HAD GAINED BOLSHEVIK MAJORITIES.

UNDER TROTSKY'S LEADERSHIP, THE PETROGRAD SOVIET ESTABLISHED ITS MILITARY REVOLUTIONARY COMMITTEE, THE FIRST STEP TOWARD A FULL-SCALE INSURRECTION.

THE SMOLNY INSTITUTE BECAME AN ARMED FORTRESS, IN PREPARATION FOR A SECOND CONGRESS OF SOVIETS LATER IN THE MONTH.

IT WAS THOUGHT THAT KERENSKY, IN HIS DESPERATION, WOULD EITHER ORDER HIS TROOPS TO RETAKE THE CITY OR ELSE ABANDON IT ALTOGETHER TO THE GERMAN ARMY, WHICH WAS STEADILY ADVANCING TOWARD PETROGRAD.

IN EITHER CASE, IT PRESENTED AN OPPORTUNITY FOR A BOLSHEVIK TAKEOVER THAT WOULD BE DEFENSIVE RATHER THAN AGGRESSIVE.

SOLDIERS AND SAILORS, ACTING INDEPENDENTLY, PUT THEMSELVES UNDER THE COMMAND OF THE MILITARY REVOLUTIONARY COMMITTEE...

...AS SUPPORT FOR THE KERENSKY GOVERNMENT DISSOLVED AWAY.

OCTOBER 24, THE DECIDING NIGHT!

THE MILITARY REVOLUTIONARY COMMITTEE WAS IN CONTINUOUS SESSION IN A SMALL ROOM AT THE SMOLNY INSTITUTE.

FOR THE ENTIRE WEEK TROTSKY HAD HARDLY STEPPED OUT OF THE BUILDING.

HE RARELY TOOK A MEAL AND SLEPT IN SNATCHES, FULLY CLOTHED, ON A LEATHER COUCH.

HE MONITORED REPORTS AS THEY POURED IN FROM ALL DISTRICTS AND SUBURBS OF THE CITY...

...ARRIVING VIA COURIER, TELEGRAM, AND TELEPHONE.

BY EVENING SOLDIERS HAD TAKEN OVER THE TELEGRAPH OFFICES, THE TELEPHONE SWITCHBOARDS, THE ELECTRICAL POWER STATIONS, AND THE POSTAL SYSTEM...

...AND HAD SECURED ALL MAJOR BRIDGES AND RAILROAD STATIONS.

IN THE EARLY-MORNING HOURS OF OCTOBER 25 THE LAST TELEPHONE MESSAGE INFORMED TROTSKY THAT ALL MAJOR POINTS OF THE CITY WERE THEIRS, WITHOUT SIGNIFICANT RESISTANCE.

HE COLLAPSED ONTO THE COUCH, FATIGUE WASHING OVER HIM.

HE ASKED LEV KAMENEV FOR A CIGARETTE.

(KAMENEV HAD BEEN OPPOSED TO THE INSURRECTION AND, THOUGH DIFFERING WITH TROTSKY POLITICALLY, WAS NOW HIS BROTHER-IN-LAW, HAVING WED HIS YOUNGER SISTER OLGA.)

AFTER TAKING ONE PUFF, HE FAINTED DEAD AWAY.

THE PROVISIONAL GOVERNMENT NOW CONSISTED OF A FEW CABINET MINISTERS COWERING INSIDE THE WINTER PALACE, THE TSAR'S FORMER RESIDENCE. KERENSKY HAD FLED THE CITY.

ON OCTOBER 25 REVOLUTIONARY TROOPS SURROUNDED THE BUILDING.

IT TOOK ONLY A FEW SOLDIERS OF THE RED GUARD TO SECURE THE PALACE AND PLACE THE MINISTERS UNDER ARREST...

...AND THE REVOLUTION WAS VICTORIOUS!

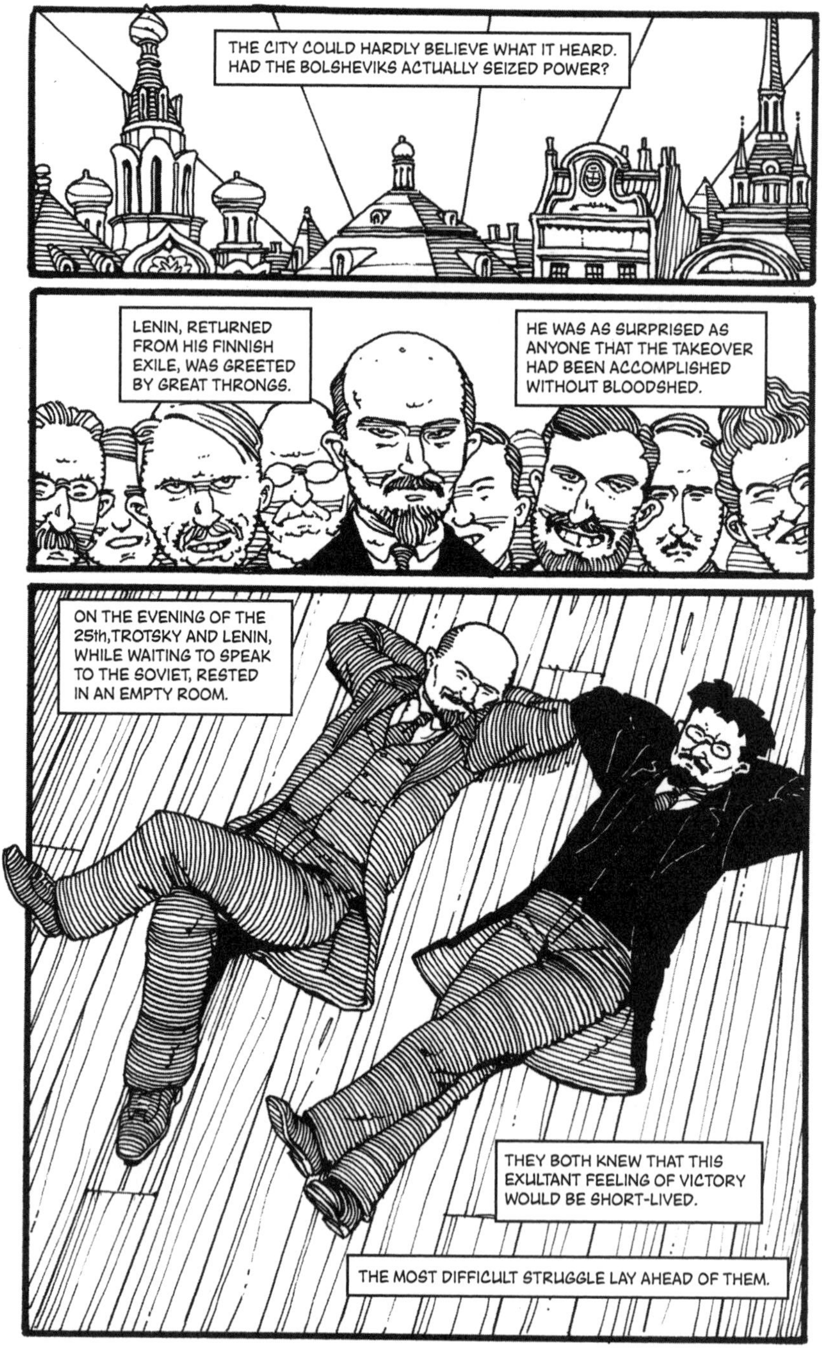
THE CITY COULD HARDLY BELIEVE WHAT IT HEARD. HAD THE BOLSHEVIKS ACTUALLY SEIZED POWER?
LENIN, RETURNED FROM HIS FINNISH EXILE, WAS GREETED BY GREAT THRONGS.
HE WAS AS SURPRISED AS ANYONE THAT THE TAKEOVER HAD BEEN ACCOMPLISHED WITHOUT BLOODSHED.
ON THE EVENING OF THE 25th,TROTSKY AND LENIN, WHILE WAITING TO SPEAK TO THE SOVIET, RESTED IN AN EMPTY ROOM.
THEY BOTH KNEW THAT THIS EXULTANT FEELING OF VICTORY WOULD BE SHORT-LIVED.
THE MOST DIFFICULT STRUGGLE LAY AHEAD OF THEM.

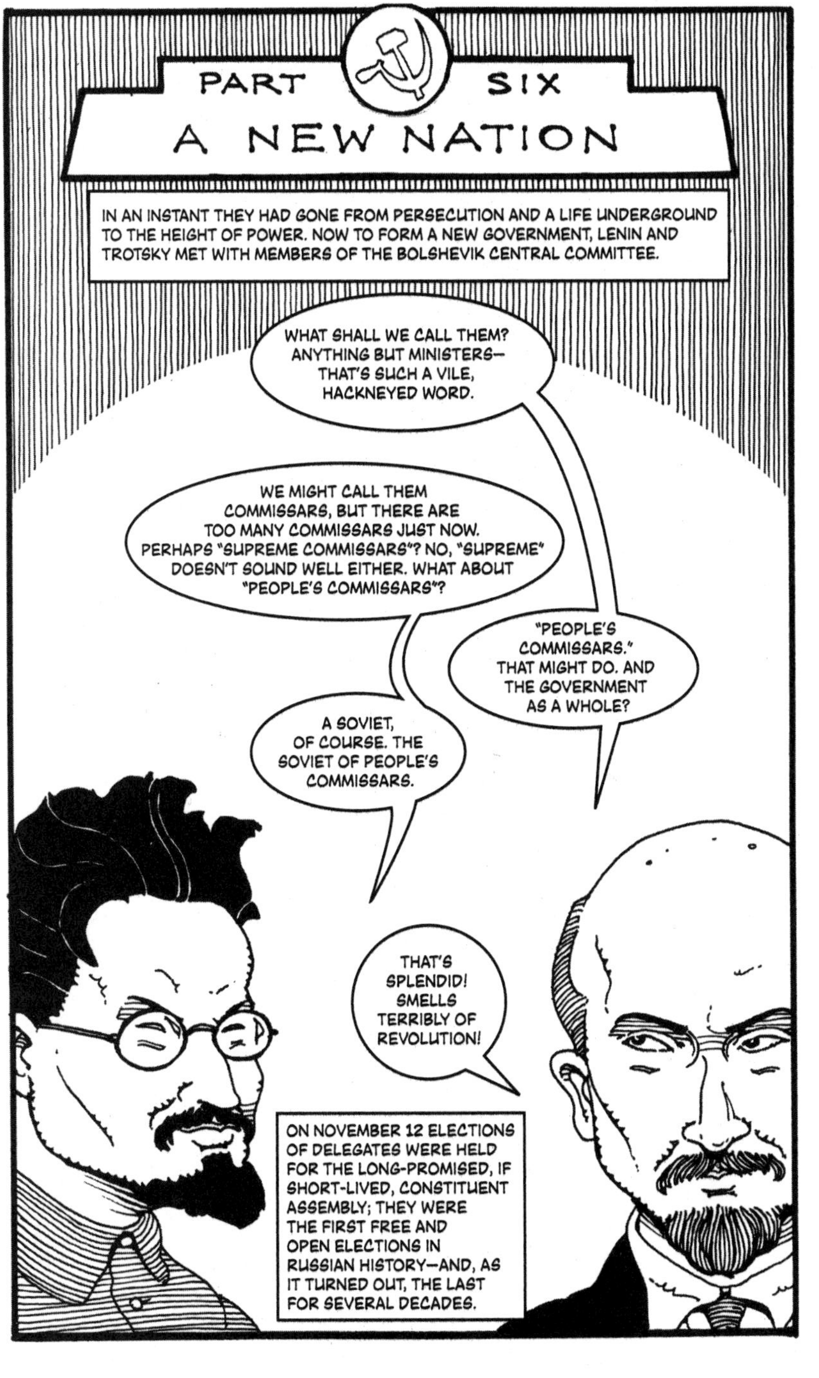
PART SIX
A NEW NATION
IN AN INSTANT THEY HAD GONE FROM PERSECUTION AND A LIFE UNDERGROUND TO THE HEIGHT OF POWER. NOW TO FORM A NEW GOVERNMENT, LENIN AND TROTSKY MET WITH MEMBERS OF THE BOLSHEVIK CENTRAL COMMITTEE.
WHAT SHALL WE CALL THEM? ANYTHING BUT MINISTERS— THAT'S SUCH A VILE, HACKNEYED WORD.
WE MIGHT CALL THEM COMMISSARS, BUT THERE ARE TOO MANY COMMISSARS JUST NOW. PERHAPS "SUPREME COMMISSARS"? NO, "SUPREME" DOESN'T SOUND WELL EITHER. WHAT ABOUT "PEOPLE'S COMMISSARS"?
"PEOPLE'S COMMISSARS." THAT MIGHT DO. AND THE GOVERNMENT AS A WHOLE?
A SOVIET, OF COURSE. THE SOVIET OF PEOPLE'S COMMISSARS.
THAT'S SPLENDID! SMELLS TERRIBLY OF REVOLUTION!
ON NOVEMBER 12 ELECTIONS OF DELEGATES WERE HELD FOR THE LONG-PROMISED, IF SHORT-LIVED, CONSTITUENT ASSEMBLY; THEY WERE THE FIRST FREE AND OPEN ELECTIONS IN RUSSIAN HISTORY—AND, AS IT TURNED OUT, THE LAST FOR SEVERAL DECADES.

LENIN WAS OF COURSE SELECTED CHAIRMAN OF THE NEW SOVIET. FOR TROTSKY, HOWEVER, THE QUESTION OF POWER WAS MORE COMPLICATED.

HE NEVER IMAGINED THAT HE WOULD TAKE PART IN THE NEW GOVERNMENT. HE WAS A WRITER, A THEORIST, A PROPAGANDIST. NEVERTHELESS, HE WAS APPOINTED COMMISSAR OF FOREIGN AFFAIRS.

SLOWLY, THROUGHOUT THE NATION, SOCIALIST REFORMS WERE ENACTED.

CLASS DISTINCTIONS WERE ABOLISHED, AND THE PROPERTIED CLASSES DISENFRANCHISED. PRIVATE OWNERSHIP OF LAND WAS ABOLISHED.

THE BANKS WERE NATIONALIZED, AND PRIVATE ENTERPRISE WAS ELIMINATED FROM THE ECONOMY.

RELIGIOUS BELIEF AND CHURCH ATTENDANCE WERE ACTIVELY DISCOURAGED.

THE CAPITAL WAS MOVED FROM SOPHISTICATED, WESTWARD-LOOKING PETROGRAD TO THE ANCIENT FORTRESS CITY OF MOSCOW.

TROTSKY MOVED HIS FAMILY INTO AN APARTMENT IN THE KREMLIN.

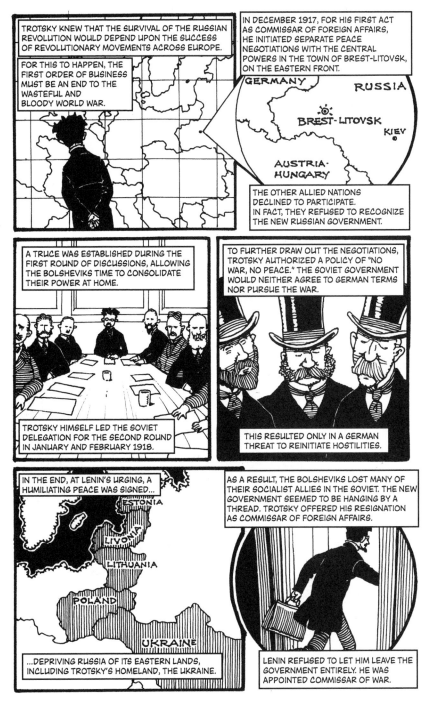

TROTSKY KNEW THAT THE SURVIVAL OF THE RUSSIAN REVOLUTION WOULD DEPEND UPON THE SUCCESS OF REVOLUTIONARY MOVEMENTS ACROSS EUROPE.

FOR THIS TO HAPPEN, THE FIRST ORDER OF BUSINESS MUST BE AN END TO THE WASTEFUL AND BLOODY WORLD WAR.

IN DECEMBER 1917, FOR HIS FIRST ACT AS COMMISSAR OF FOREIGN AFFAIRS, HE INITIATED SEPARATE PEACE NEGOTIATIONS WITH THE CENTRAL POWERS IN THE TOWN OF BREST-LITOVSK, ON THE EASTERN FRONT.

GERMANY

RUSSIA

BREST-LITOVSK

KIEV

AUSTRIA-HUNGARY

THE OTHER ALLIED NATIONS DECLINED TO PARTICIPATE. IN FACT, THEY REFUSED TO RECOGNIZE THE NEW RUSSIAN GOVERNMENT.

A TRUCE WAS ESTABLISHED DURING THE FIRST ROUND OF DISCUSSIONS, ALLOWING THE BOLSHEVIKS TIME TO CONSOLIDATE THEIR POWER AT HOME.

TROTSKY HIMSELF LED THE SOVIET DELEGATION FOR THE SECOND ROUND IN JANUARY AND FEBRUARY 1918.

TO FURTHER DRAW OUT THE NEGOTIATIONS, TROTSKY AUTHORIZED A POLICY OF "NO WAR, NO PEACE." THE SOVIET GOVERNMENT WOULD NEITHER AGREE TO GERMAN TERMS NOR PURSUE THE WAR.

THIS RESULTED ONLY IN A GERMAN THREAT TO REINITIATE HOSTILITIES.

IN THE END, AT LENIN'S URGING, A HUMILIATING PEACE WAS SIGNED...

ESTONIA

LIVONIA

LITHUANIA

POLAND

UKRAINE

...DEPRIVING RUSSIA OF ITS EASTERN LANDS, INCLUDING TROTSKY'S HOMELAND, THE UKRAINE.

AS A RESULT, THE BOLSHEVIKS LOST MANY OF THEIR SOCIALIST ALLIES IN THE SOVIET. THE NEW GOVERNMENT SEEMED TO BE HANGING BY A THREAD. TROTSKY OFFERED HIS RESIGNATION AS COMMISSAR OF FOREIGN AFFAIRS.

LENIN REFUSED TO LET HIM LEAVE THE GOVERNMENT ENTIRELY. HE WAS APPOINTED COMMISSAR OF WAR.

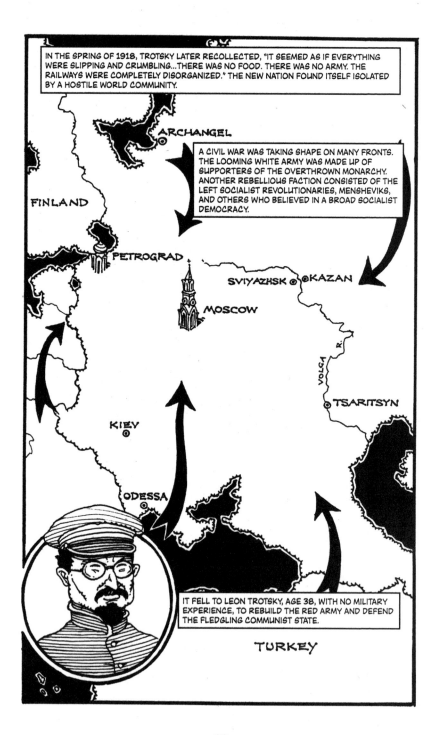

IN THE SPRING OF 1918, TROTSKY LATER RECOLLECTED, "IT SEEMED AS IF EVERYTHING WERE SLIPPING AND CRUMBLING...THERE WAS NO FOOD. THERE WAS NO ARMY. THE RAILWAYS WERE COMPLETELY DISORGANIZED." THE NEW NATION FOUND ITSELF ISOLATED BY A HOSTILE WORLD COMMUNITY.

ARCHANGEL

A CIVIL WAR WAS TAKING SHAPE ON MANY FRONTS. THE LOOMING WHITE ARMY WAS MADE UP OF SUPPORTERS OF THE OVERTHROWN MONARCHY. ANOTHER REBELLIOUS FACTION CONSISTED OF THE LEFT SOCIALIST REVOLUTIONARIES, MENSHEVIKS, AND OTHERS WHO BELIEVED IN A BROAD SOCIALIST DEMOCRACY.

FINLAND

PETROGRAD

SVIYAZHSK ● ●KAZAN

MOSCOW

VOLGA R.

TSARITSYN

KIEV

ODESSA

IT FELL TO LEON TROTSKY, AGE 38, WITH NO MILITARY EXPERIENCE, TO REBUILD THE RED ARMY AND DEFEND THE FLEDGLING COMMUNIST STATE.

TURKEY

TO CARRY HIM TO THE VARIOUS CENTERS OF BATTLE, TROTSKY ORDERED THE OUTFITTING OF A SPECIAL TRAIN.

IT WOULD BE HIS HOME FOR THE NEXT TWO AND A HALF YEARS, AND DURING THAT TIME IT WOULD GROW INTO AN IMPOSING FORTRESS.

SO HEAVILY ARMORED IT NEEDED TWO ENGINES TO PULL IT, THE TRAIN WAS MANNED BY A LOYAL CREW. IT HOUSED RADIO AND TELEGRAPH STATIONS, A PRINTING PRESS, AN ELECTRIC POWER PLANT, OFFICES, A LIBRARY, TRUCKS, CARS, AND AIRCRAFT.

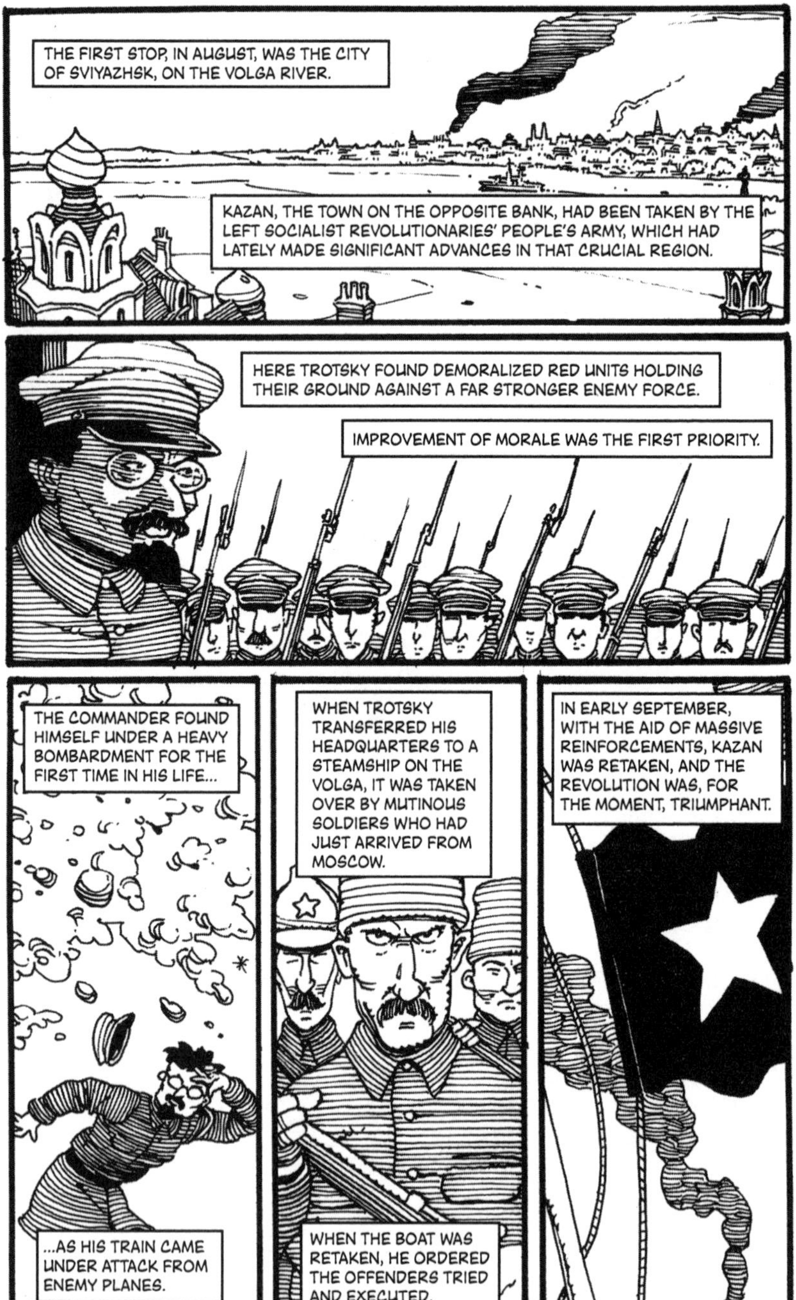
THE FIRST STOP, IN AUGUST, WAS THE CITY OF SVIYAZHSK, ON THE VOLGA RIVER.
KAZAN, THE TOWN ON THE OPPOSITE BANK, HAD BEEN TAKEN BY THE LEFT SOCIALIST REVOLUTIONARIES' PEOPLE'S ARMY, WHICH HAD LATELY MADE SIGNIFICANT ADVANCES IN THAT CRUCIAL REGION.
HERE TROTSKY FOUND DEMORALIZED RED UNITS HOLDING THEIR GROUND AGAINST A FAR STRONGER ENEMY FORCE.
IMPROVEMENT OF MORALE WAS THE FIRST PRIORITY.
THE COMMANDER FOUND HIMSELF UNDER A HEAVY BOMBARDMENT FOR THE FIRST TIME IN HIS LIFE...
...AS HIS TRAIN CAME UNDER ATTACK FROM ENEMY PLANES.
WHEN TROTSKY TRANSFERRED HIS HEADQUARTERS TO A STEAMSHIP ON THE VOLGA, IT WAS TAKEN OVER BY MUTINOUS SOLDIERS WHO HAD JUST ARRIVED FROM MOSCOW.
WHEN THE BOAT WAS RETAKEN, HE ORDERED THE OFFENDERS TRIED AND EXECUTED.
IN EARLY SEPTEMBER, WITH THE AID OF MASSIVE REINFORCEMENTS, KAZAN WAS RETAKEN, AND THE REVOLUTION WAS, FOR THE MOMENT, TRIUMPHANT.

ON HIS MISSIONS TO THE FRONT LINES, TROTSKY FOUND SEVERE SHORTAGES OF ARMS AND SUPPLIES, AND HIGH RATES OF INSUBORDINATION AND DESERTION.

HIS SKILLS AT PLANNING AND ORGANIZATION RECEIVED THEIR SEVEREST CHALLENGE.

HE RALLIED THE TROOPS WITH INSPIRATIONAL SPEECHES AND OFFERED REWARDS FOR OUTSTANDING SERVICE.

HE BROUGHT IN DOCTORS, DENTISTS, EVEN A BAND.

HE WAS ALSO NOT OPPOSED TO RUTHLESS MEANS OF IMPOSING DISCIPLINE.

DESERTERS WERE PUT TO DEATH. EVERY TENTH MAN WAS EXECUTED FROM UNITS THAT REFUSED TO FIGHT.

ALL THE WHILE HE WAS THE FACE OF THE RED ARMY, ITS PUBLIC SYMBOL...

...EXPOSING HIMSELF, TIME AFTER TIME, TO ENEMY FIRE.

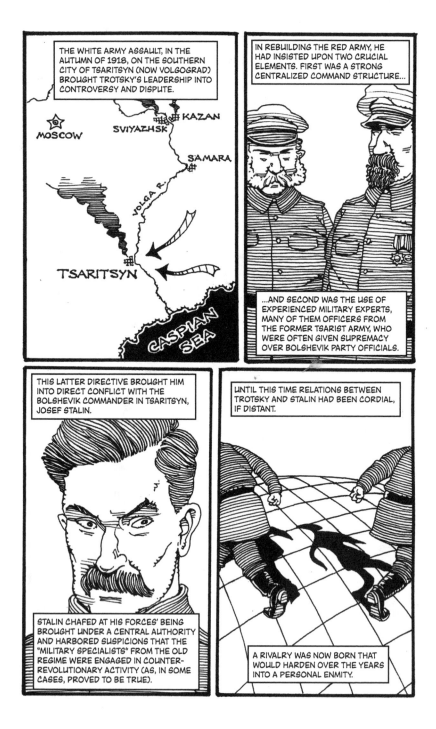

THE WHITE ARMY ASSAULT, IN THE AUTUMN OF 1918, ON THE SOUTHERN CITY OF TSARITSYN (NOW VOLGOGRAD) BROUGHT TROTSKY'S LEADERSHIP INTO CONTROVERSY AND DISPUTE.

MOSCOW

KAZAN

SVIYAZHSK

SAMARA

VOLGA R.

TSARITSYN

CASPIAN SEA

IN REBUILDING THE RED ARMY, HE HAD INSISTED UPON TWO CRUCIAL ELEMENTS. FIRST WAS A STRONG CENTRALIZED COMMAND STRUCTURE...

...AND SECOND WAS THE USE OF EXPERIENCED MILITARY EXPERTS, MANY OF THEM OFFICERS FROM THE FORMER TSARIST ARMY, WHO WERE OFTEN GIVEN SUPREMACY OVER BOLSHEVIK PARTY OFFICIALS.

THIS LATTER DIRECTIVE BROUGHT HIM INTO DIRECT CONFLICT WITH THE BOLSHEVIK COMMANDER IN TSARITSYN, JOSEF STALIN.

STALIN CHAFED AT HIS FORCES' BEING BROUGHT UNDER A CENTRAL AUTHORITY AND HARBORED SUSPICIONS THAT THE "MILITARY SPECIALISTS" FROM THE OLD REGIME WERE ENGAGED IN COUNTER-REVOLUTIONARY ACTIVITY (AS, IN SOME CASES, PROVED TO BE TRUE).

UNTIL THIS TIME RELATIONS BETWEEN TROTSKY AND STALIN HAD BEEN CORDIAL, IF DISTANT.

A RIVALRY WAS NOW BORN THAT WOULD HARDEN OVER THE YEARS INTO A PERSONAL ENMITY.

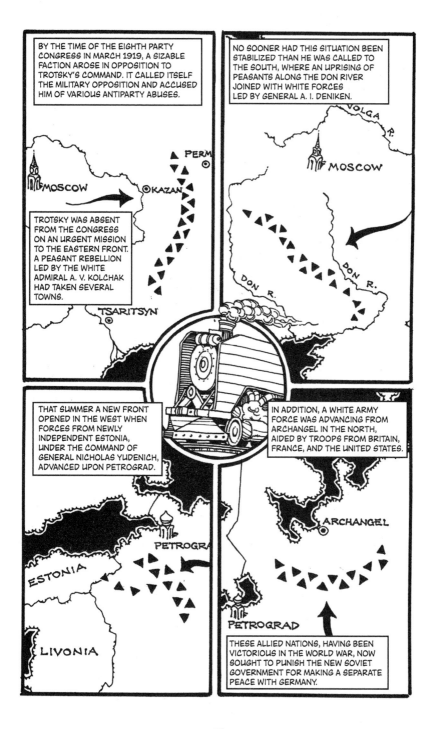

BY THE TIME OF THE EIGHTH PARTY CONGRESS IN MARCH 1919, A SIZABLE FACTION AROSE IN OPPOSITION TO TROTSKY'S COMMAND. IT CALLED ITSELF THE MILITARY OPPOSITION AND ACCUSED HIM OF VARIOUS ANTIPARTY ABUSES.

TROTSKY WAS ABSENT FROM THE CONGRESS ON AN URGENT MISSION TO THE EASTERN FRONT. A PEASANT REBELLION LED BY THE WHITE ADMIRAL A. V. KOLCHAK HAD TAKEN SEVERAL TOWNS.

PERM

MOSCOW

KAZAN

TSARITSYN

NO SOONER HAD THIS SITUATION BEEN STABILIZED THAN HE WAS CALLED TO THE SOUTH, WHERE AN UPRISING OF PEASANTS ALONG THE DON RIVER JOINED WITH WHITE FORCES LED BY GENERAL A. I. DENIKEN.

VOLGA R.

MOSCOW

DON R.

DON R.

THAT SUMMER A NEW FRONT OPENED IN THE WEST WHEN FORCES FROM NEWLY INDEPENDENT ESTONIA, UNDER THE COMMAND OF GENERAL NICHOLAS YUDENICH, ADVANCED UPON PETROGRAD.

PETROGRA

ESTONIA

LIVONIA

IN ADDITION, A WHITE ARMY FORCE WAS ADVANCING FROM ARCHANGEL IN THE NORTH, AIDED BY TROOPS FROM BRITAIN, FRANCE, AND THE UNITED STATES.

ARCHANGEL

PETROGRAD

THESE ALLIED NATIONS, HAVING BEEN VICTORIOUS IN THE WORLD WAR, NOW SOUGHT TO PUNISH THE NEW SOVIET GOVERNMENT FOR MAKING A SEPARATE PEACE WITH GERMANY.

ALTHOUGH LENIN AND OTHERS ADVISED SURRENDERING PETROGRAD, TROTSKY WENT THERE IN OCTOBER AND LED THE CITY'S DEFENSE.

ON HORSEBACK, BULLETS WHIZZING ABOUT HIM, HE TURNED BACK A REGIMENT OF RETREATING SOLDIERS.

FOR THE REMAINDER OF 1919 AND INTO 1920, THE RED ARMY REMAINED ON THE OFFENSIVE.

ВОЙНА
ПОБѢДНАГО

THE WHITE FORCES AND THEIR ALLIES WERE TURNED BACK AND, FACED WITH SUPERIOR NUMBERS, EVENTUALLY ROUTED.

ALTHOUGH, OVER THE NEXT TWO YEARS, LOCALIZED REBELLIONS BROKE OUT, THE CIVIL WAR WAS NOW EFFECTIVELY AT AN END...

...AND THE YOUNG GOVERNMENT COULD TURN ITS ATTENTION TO REBUILDING THE NATION.

AFTER ALMOST SIX YEARS OF WAR, MORE THAN 20 MILLION RUSSIANS WERE DEAD...

...AND THOSE WHO SURVIVED FACED WIDESPREAD SHORTAGES OF FOOD AND FUEL. INDUSTRIAL AND AGRICULTURAL OUTPUT WAS AT A LOW POINT.

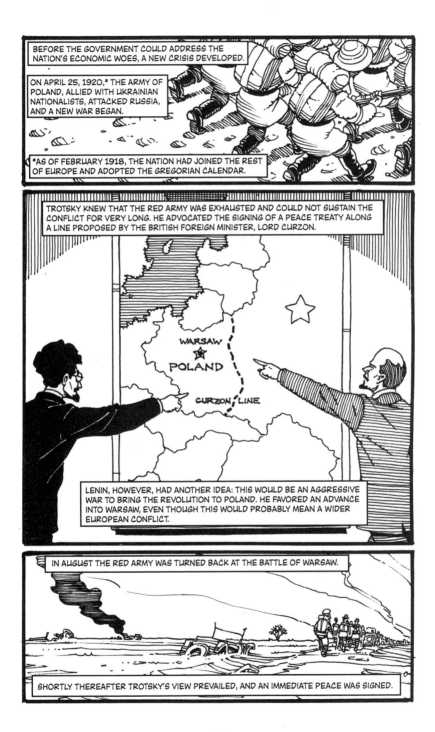

BEFORE THE GOVERNMENT COULD ADDRESS THE NATION'S ECONOMIC WOES, A NEW CRISIS DEVELOPED.

ON APRIL 25, 1920,* THE ARMY OF POLAND, ALLIED WITH UKRAINIAN NATIONALISTS, ATTACKED RUSSIA, AND A NEW WAR BEGAN.

*AS OF FEBRUARY 1918, THE NATION HAD JOINED THE REST OF EUROPE AND ADOPTED THE GREGORIAN CALENDAR.

TROTSKY KNEW THAT THE RED ARMY WAS EXHAUSTED AND COULD NOT SUSTAIN THE CONFLICT FOR VERY LONG. HE ADVOCATED THE SIGNING OF A PEACE TREATY ALONG A LINE PROPOSED BY THE BRITISH FOREIGN MINISTER, LORD CURZON.

WARSAW
POLAND
CURZON LINE

LENIN, HOWEVER, HAD ANOTHER IDEA: THIS WOULD BE AN AGGRESSIVE WAR TO BRING THE REVOLUTION TO POLAND. HE FAVORED AN ADVANCE INTO WARSAW, EVEN THOUGH THIS WOULD PROBABLY MEAN A WIDER EUROPEAN CONFLICT.

IN AUGUST THE RED ARMY WAS TURNED BACK AT THE BATTLE OF WARSAW.

SHORTLY THEREAFTER TROTSKY'S VIEW PREVAILED, AND AN IMMEDIATE PEACE WAS SIGNED.

ALTHOUGH TROTSKY WAS NOW NATIONALLY RECOGNIZED AS THE HERO OF THE CIVIL WAR AND SAVIOR OF THE REVOLUTION, HE STILL OCCUPIED A SHAKY POLITICAL POSITION. HIS SKILLS AS AN ADMINISTRATOR, HOWEVER, COULD NOT BE IGNORED.

IN 1919 HE HAD BEEN ELECTED TO THE NEWLY FORMED POLITBURO, THE RULING EXECUTIVE COMMITTEE OF THE COMMUNIST PARTY (AS THE BOLSHEVIKS NOW CALLED THEMSELVES), ALONG WITH LENIN, STALIN, KAMENEV, AND NICHOLAS KRESTINSKY.

IN ADDITION TO HIS POSITION AS COMMISSAR OF WAR, HE WAS APPOINTED COMMISSAR OF TRANSPORT...

...WITH THE IMMEDIATE TASK OF REBUILDING THE NATION'S CRUMBLING RAIL INFRASTRUCTURE.

HE OBSERVED THAT "ALL THE FUNDAMENTAL QUESTIONS OF SOCIALIST ORGANIZATION OF ECONOMIC LIFE FOUND THEIR MOST CONCENTRATED EXPRESSION IN THE SPHERE OF TRANSPORT."

HE FOUNDED TSEKTRAN, A TRADE UNION FOR ALL TRANSPORT WORKERS, CHAIRED BY HIM AND UNDER DIRECT PARTY CONTROL.

IN ECONOMIC AS IN MILITARY MATTERS, TROTSKY ADVOCATED THOROUGH PLANNING AND STRONG CENTRALIZED AUTHORITY...

...AS WELL AS THE RECRUITMENT OF "EXPERTS," OFTEN IN THE FORM OF INDUSTRIALISTS FROM THE FORMER CAPITALIST SYSTEM.

FOR ECONOMIC RECOVERY, HE ENVISIONED A LABOR ARMY, STRUCTURED LIKE THE MILITARY AND BUILT THROUGH UNIVERSAL CONSCRIPTION.

A CENSUS WOULD BE TAKEN, MARKING EACH MAN'S TRADE AND PRODUCTIVE SKILLS, AND THEN EACH WOULD BE SENT TO THE LOCATION WHERE HIS SKILLS WERE NEEDED.

HIS VIEWS BROUGHT HIM INTO CONFLICT WITH THE NATION'S POWERFUL TRADE UNIONS.

TROTSKY BELIEVED THAT IN A SOCIALIST STATE THE NEED FOR UNIONS WOULD DIMINISH, AND THEY WOULD BECOME ORGANS OF THE GOVERNMENT. HIS UNION TSEKTRAN WOULD BE THE MODEL FOR OTHERS.

LENIN, HOWEVER, BELIEVED THAT THE UNIONS SHOULD CONTINUE AS AUTONOMOUS ORGANIZATIONS—YET ANOTHER POINT OF CONTENTION BETWEEN HIM AND TROTSKY.

LENIN PLACED ZINOVIEV IN CHARGE OF ALL TRADE UNION MATTERS.

GROWING CIVIL UNREST REACHED A PEAK IN THE EARLY MONTHS OF 1921 WITH A MUTINY OF SAILORS AT THE KRONSTADT NAVAL BASE OUTSIDE PETROGRAD.

WITH THE APPROVAL OF THE COMMISSAR OF WAR, THE REBELLION WAS VIOLENTLY PUT DOWN BY ASSAULT OF THE RED ARMY.

LENIN'S ONE-PARTY STATE HAD SHOWN THAT IT WOULD BROOK NO POLITICAL OPPOSITION; EVEN LEFTIST PARTIES LIKE THE SOCIALIST REVOLUTIONARIES AND THE MENSHEVIKS WERE ABOLISHED.

BUT IT COULD STILL BE FLEXIBLE IN REGARD TO THE ECONOMIC DEMANDS OF THE MASSES. A NEW ECONOMIC PLAN WAS ENACTED TO PERMIT FREE TRADE IN AGRICULTURE AND SMALL-SCALE PRIVATE ENTERPRISE.

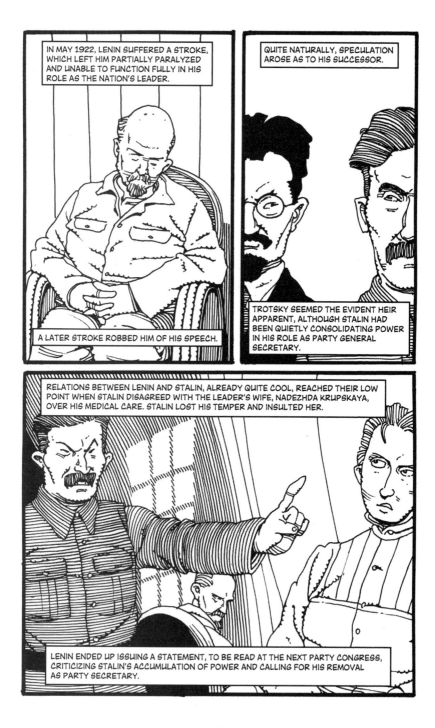

IN MAY 1922, LENIN SUFFERED A STROKE, WHICH LEFT HIM PARTIALLY PARALYZED AND UNABLE TO FUNCTION FULLY IN HIS ROLE AS THE NATION'S LEADER.

A LATER STROKE ROBBED HIM OF HIS SPEECH.

QUITE NATURALLY, SPECULATION AROSE AS TO HIS SUCCESSOR.

TROTSKY SEEMED THE EVIDENT HEIR APPARENT, ALTHOUGH STALIN HAD BEEN QUIETLY CONSOLIDATING POWER IN HIS ROLE AS PARTY GENERAL SECRETARY.

RELATIONS BETWEEN LENIN AND STALIN, ALREADY QUITE COOL, REACHED THEIR LOW POINT WHEN STALIN DISAGREED WITH THE LEADER'S WIFE, NADEZHDA KRUPSKAYA, OVER HIS MEDICAL CARE. STALIN LOST HIS TEMPER AND INSULTED HER.

LENIN ENDED UP ISSUING A STATEMENT, TO BE READ AT THE NEXT PARTY CONGRESS, CRITICIZING STALIN'S ACCUMULATION OF POWER AND CALLING FOR HIS REMOVAL AS PARTY SECRETARY.

PART ⚒ SEVEN

FALL FROM POWER

NIKOLAI LENIN DIED ON JANUARY 21, 1924, AT AGE 53.

TROTSKY WAS PARTICULARLY HORRIFIED THAT HIS REMAINS WERE PUT ON DISPLAY IN A GRAND MAUSOLEUM IN MOSCOW'S RED SQUARE. HE OPPOSED SUCH DEIFICATION AS "UNBECOMING AND OFFENSIVE TO THE REVOLUTIONARY CONSCIOUSNESS."

THE NEXT FOUR YEARS SAW THE INCREASING MARGINALIZATION OF TROTSKY WITHIN THE GOVERNMENT AND THE PARTY.

RUSSIA HAD BY NOW ABSORBED ITS INTERNAL ENTITIES INTO ONE VAST NATION, THE UNION OF SOVIET SOCIALIST REPUBLICS.

THE CITY OF PETROGRAD WAS RENAMED LENINGRAD.

LENIN'S SUCCESSOR WAS A TOPIC OF HEATED DISCUSSION.

THE DYING LEADER'S DECLARATION OPPOSING STALIN WAS UNCLEAR ON THIS SUBJECT; HE DID NOT PROMOTE TROTSKY ABOVE ANY OTHER COMRADE.

STALIN, KAMENEV, AND ZINOVIEV FORMED A TROIKA IN OPPOSITION TO TROTSKY.

AS THE PARTY CLOSED RANKS, IT WOULD TOLERATE NO FACTIONS OR ANY KIND OF INTERNAL OPPOSITION.

STALIN'S RISE TO POWER CONTINUED UNABATED WITHIN A NEW BUREAUCRACY DEDICATED SOLELY TO ITS OWN PERPETUATION.

TROTSKY WAS TO DEDICATE HIMSELF TO FIGHTING WHAT HE SAW AS A NEW "THERMIDOR," A TERM IN REFERENCE TO THE PERIOD OF REACTION FOLLOWING THE FRENCH REVOLUTION.

IT DENOTED A SWING OF THE PENDULUM BACK TO A MORE CONSERVATIVE, STABILITY-SEEKING MIND-SET. IN FRANCE IT HAD LED TO THE RISE OF NAPOLEON BONAPARTE.

IN JANUARY 1925, TROTSKY WAS REMOVED FROM HIS POST AS WAR COMMISSAR...

...AND THEREAFTER GIVEN ONLY MINOR ADMINISTRATIVE POSITIONS.

SUCH POSTS AS CHAIRMAN OF THE CONCESSIONS COMMITTEE, HEAD OF THE ELECTROTECHNICAL BOARD, CHAIRMAN OF THE SCIENTIFIC-TECHNICAL BOARD OF INDUSTRY HE FULFILLED WITH ENTHUSIASM...

...ALTHOUGH, AS HE LATER SAID, HE WAS ASSIGNED THEM "TO ISOLATE ME FROM THE PARTY, TO SUBMERGE ME IN ROUTINE."

HIS ENEMIES CITED HIS ABRASIVE PERSONALITY AS AN IMPEDIMENT TO WORKING RELATIONS...

...HIS ARROGANCE, AND HIS RUTHLESSNESS TOWARD SUBORDINATES.

THE FAILED REVOLUTION IN GERMANY IN OCTOBER 1923...

...AND THE DEFEAT OF THE BRITISH GENERAL STRIKE IN 1926...

...LED TROTSKY TO REALIZE THAT SOVIET POWER COULD NO LONGER DEPEND UPON WORLDWIDE REVOLUTION.

THE PERIOD OF REACTION WAS IN FULL SWING AS STALIN INSTITUTED A POLICY OF "SOCIALISM IN ONE COUNTRY."

AN AMBITIOUS FIVE-YEAR PLAN, A MASSIVE GREAT LEAP FORWARD, WAS PUT IN PLACE TO IMPROVE INDUSTRIAL OUTPUT.

TROTSKY COULD PARTICIPATE IN THIS DEBATE ONLY FITFULLY...

...AS MYSTERIOUSLY RECURRING FEVERS KEPT HIM OUT OF COMMISSION FOR WEEKS AT A TIME.

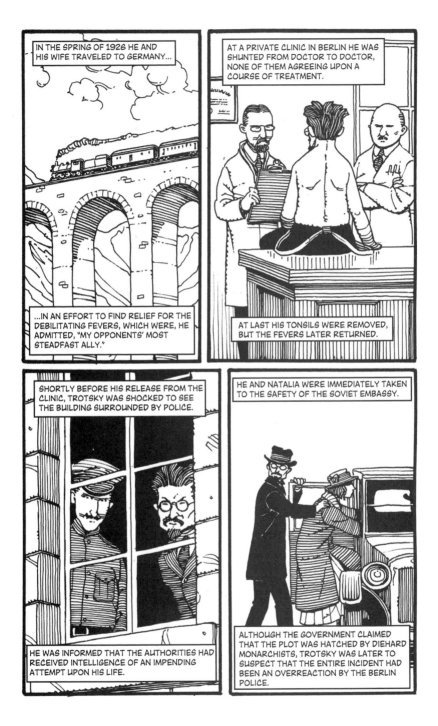

IN THE SPRING OF 1926 HE AND HIS WIFE TRAVELED TO GERMANY...

...IN AN EFFORT TO FIND RELIEF FOR THE DEBILITATING FEVERS, WHICH WERE, HE ADMITTED, "MY OPPONENTS' MOST STEADFAST ALLY."

AT A PRIVATE CLINIC IN BERLIN HE WAS SHUNTED FROM DOCTOR TO DOCTOR, NONE OF THEM AGREEING UPON A COURSE OF TREATMENT.

AT LAST HIS TONSILS WERE REMOVED, BUT THE FEVERS LATER RETURNED.

SHORTLY BEFORE HIS RELEASE FROM THE CLINIC, TROTSKY WAS SHOCKED TO SEE THE BUILDING SURROUNDED BY POLICE.

HE WAS INFORMED THAT THE AUTHORITIES HAD RECEIVED INTELLIGENCE OF AN IMPENDING ATTEMPT UPON HIS LIFE.

HE AND NATALIA WERE IMMEDIATELY TAKEN TO THE SAFETY OF THE SOVIET EMBASSY.

ALTHOUGH THE GOVERNMENT CLAIMED THAT THE PLOT WAS HATCHED BY DIEHARD MONARCHISTS, TROTSKY WAS LATER TO SUSPECT THAT THE ENTIRE INCIDENT HAD BEEN AN OVERREACTION BY THE BERLIN POLICE.

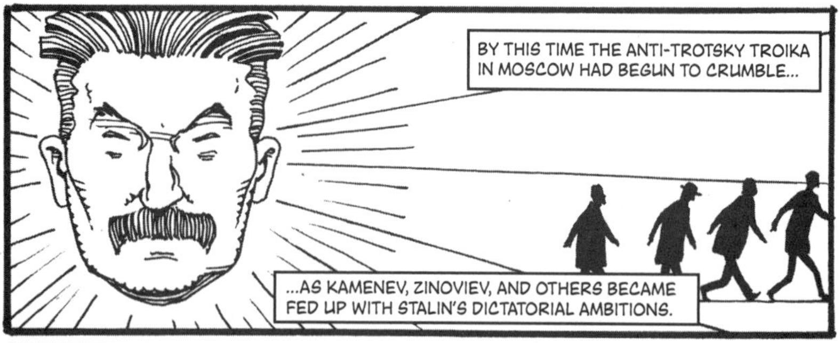
BY THIS TIME THE ANTI-TROTSKY TROIKA IN MOSCOW HAD BEGUN TO CRUMBLE...
...AS KAMENEV, ZINOVIEV, AND OTHERS BECAME FED UP WITH STALIN'S DICTATORIAL AMBITIONS.

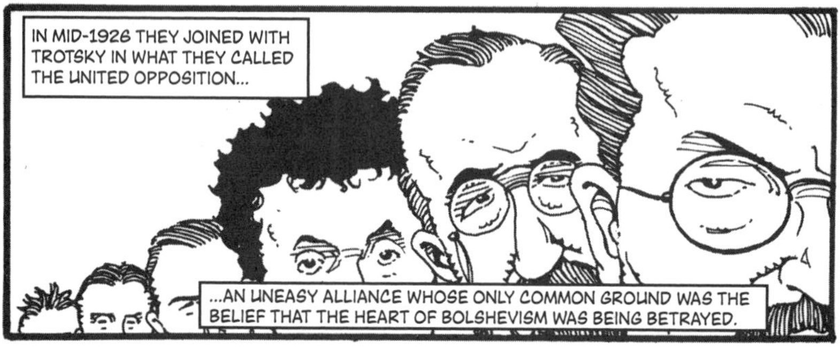
IN MID-1926 THEY JOINED WITH TROTSKY IN WHAT THEY CALLED THE UNITED OPPOSITION...
...AN UNEASY ALLIANCE WHOSE ONLY COMMON GROUND WAS THE BELIEF THAT THE HEART OF BOLSHEVISM WAS BEING BETRAYED.

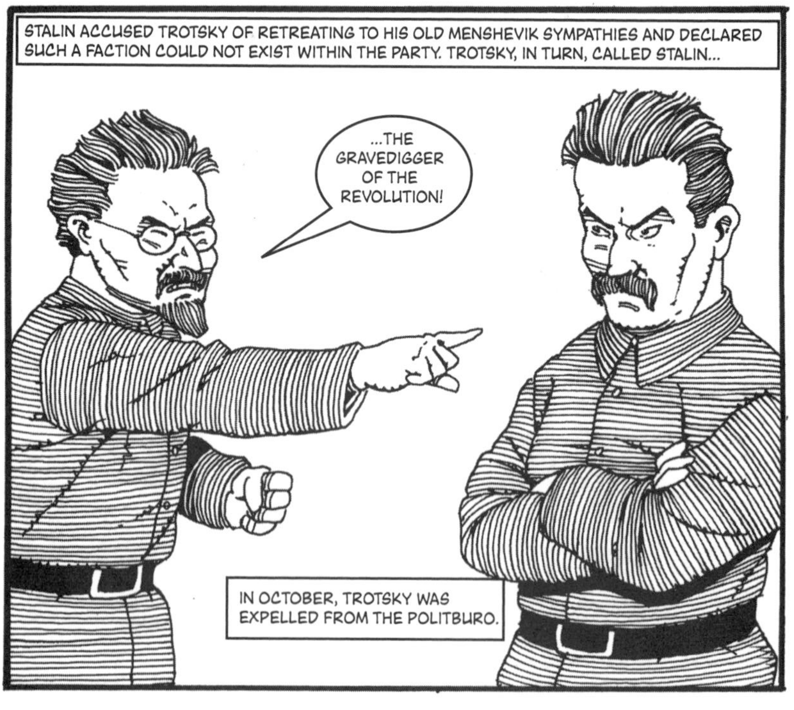
STALIN ACCUSED TROTSKY OF RETREATING TO HIS OLD MENSHEVIK SYMPATHIES AND DECLARED SUCH A FACTION COULD NOT EXIST WITHIN THE PARTY. TROTSKY, IN TURN, CALLED STALIN...
...THE GRAVEDIGGER OF THE REVOLUTION!
IN OCTOBER, TROTSKY WAS EXPELLED FROM THE POLITBURO.

THROUGHOUT 1925 AND 1926, A MAJOR POINT OF DISAGREEMENT BETWEEN THE SOVIET LEADERSHIP AND THE UNITED OPPOSITION CONCERNED THE NEWLY FORMED CHINESE COMMUNIST PARTY—AND ITS ROLE IN THE SIMMERING NATIONALIST REVOLT AGAINST THE FEUDAL WARLORDS WHO CONTROLLED THEIR COUNTRY.

MONGOLIA

MANCHURIA

SINKIANG

PEIPING (BEIJING)

CHINA

TIBET

SHANGHAI

INDIA

STALIN PROPOSED THAT THE COMMUNISTS REMAIN WITHIN THE RANKS OF THE NATIONALIST ARMY (KNOWN AS THE KUOMINTANG), LED BY GENERAL CHIANG KAI-SHEK, THE BETTER TO ADVANCE THEIR POSITION AFTER A NATIONALIST VICTORY.

TROTSKY AND THE OPPOSITION CALLED FOR THE COMMUNISTS TO RETAIN THEIR INDEPENDENCE...

...AND ESTABLISH SOVIETS OF WORKERS' DEPUTIES WITHIN CHINESE INDUSTRIAL CENTERS.

STALIN'S POSITION PREVAILED, AND THE USSR SENT MASSIVE MILITARY AID TO THE NATIONALISTS.

HOWEVER, WHEN THE KUOMINTANG CAME TO POWER IN THE SPRING OF 1927, CHIANG KAI-SHEK SET ABOUT THE SYSTEMATIC SLAUGHTER OF THE COMMUNIST PARTY.

AS 1927 DREW TO A CLOSE, STALIN AND HIS "APPARATUS" PREPARED FOR A BLOODY SETTLEMENT OF THEIR CONFLICT WITH THE OPPOSITION.

ACCORDING TO TROTSKY, THE PARTY NOW FELT ITSELF AT A CROSSROADS.

SECRET MEETINGS, PACKED BY YOUNG WORKERS AND STUDENTS EAGER TO HEAR THE OPPOSITION MESSAGE, WERE HELD IN SEVERAL CITIES.

ON NOVEMBER 7, OPPOSITION-ORGANIZED MASS DEMONSTRATIONS TOOK PLACE IN MOSCOW AND LENINGRAD, TO COMMEMORATE THE TENTH ANNIVERSARY OF THE BOLSHEVIK REVOLUTION.

THEIR PLACARDS READ: "LET US CARRY OUT LENIN'S WILL" AND "FOR THE UNITY OF LENIN'S PARTY."

SPECIALLY RECRUITED POLICE UNITS ATTACKED THE DEMONSTRATORS, TORE UP THEIR PLACARDS...

...AND PUMMELED THOSE WHO RESISTED.

STALIN MADE HIS FINAL MOVE AT THE 15th PARTY CONGRESS IN DECEMBER.

THE LEADERSHIP OF THE OPPOSITION—TROTSKY, KAMENEV, AND ZINOVIEV—HAD ALREADY MADE A SMALL CAPITULATION: THOUGH THEY COULD NOT RECANT THEIR VIEWS, THEY WOULD FORGO FACTIONAL ACTIVITY FOR THE SAKE OF PARTY UNITY.

NEVERTHELESS, ALL THREE, ALONG WITH THEIR FOLLOWERS, WERE EXPELLED FROM THE PARTY.

KAMENEV AND ZINOVIEV SOON REVERSED THEIR POSITIONS AND WERE MERELY GIVEN A SIX-MONTH PROBATION.

BUT LEON TROTSKY REFUSED TO RECANT...

...AND, FOR THE THIRD TIME IN HIS LIFE, WAS ORDERED TO INTERNAL EXILE.

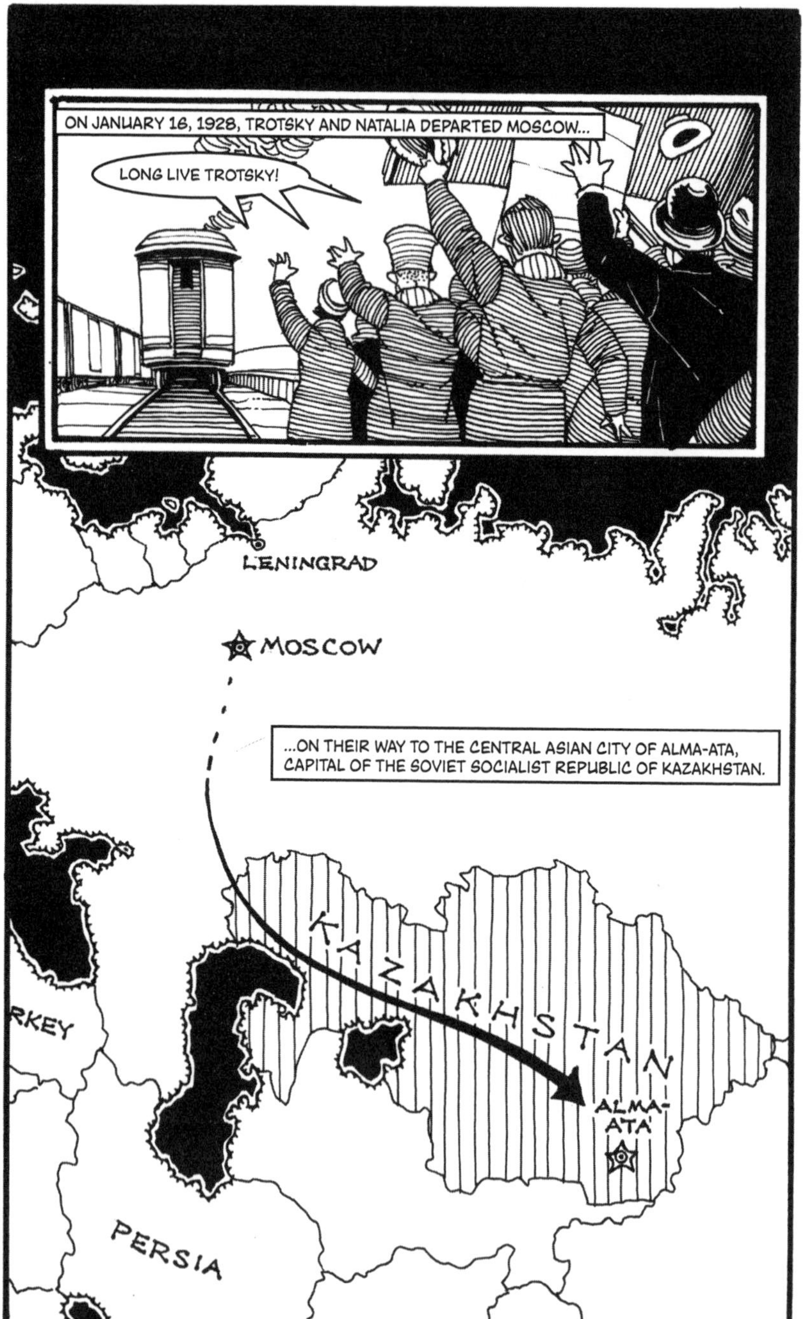
ON JANUARY 16, 1928, TROTSKY AND NATALIA DEPARTED MOSCOW...
LONG LIVE TROTSKY!
LENINGRAD
MOSCOW
...ON THEIR WAY TO THE CENTRAL ASIAN CITY OF ALMA-ATA, CAPITAL OF THE SOVIET SOCIALIST REPUBLIC OF KAZAKHSTAN.
KAZAKHSTAN
ALMA-ATA
RKEY
PERSIA

PART EIGHT
THE FINAL EXILE

DURING HIS YEAR IN ALMA-ATA, TROTSKY KEPT IN CLOSE CONTACT WITH HIS SUPPORTERS IN MOSCOW AND LENINGRAD...

...AND HE HEARD WITH DISMAY THAT FORMER ALLIES—KAMENEV, ZINOVIEV, AND OTHERS OF THE OPPOSITION—HAD RENOUNCED THEIR PRINCIPLES AND BEEN WELCOMED BACK INTO THE PARTY.

FROM HIS LITTLE DACHA, HE WROTE PRODIGIOUSLY, PRODUCING A BOOK OF MEMOIRS, *MY LIFE*, AND BEGINNING AN AMBITIOUS MULTIVOLUME *HISTORY OF THE RUSSIAN REVOLUTION*...

...IN ADDITION TO A CASCADE OF ARTICLES AND ESSAYS DENOUNCING STALIN WHILE MAINTAINING TROTSKY'S LOYALTY TO THE PRINCIPLES OF THE PARTY.

LIFE IN THE PROVINCIAL CITY WAS DIFFICULT, WITH HARSH WINTERS AND SCORCHING SUMMERS. TROTSKY CALLED IT "A REALM OF HORRIFYING DUST."

SWARMING MOSQUITOES BROUGHT ON BOUTS OF MALARIA.

DURING THIS TIME TROTSKY LEARNED OF THE DEATH, FROM TUBERCULOSIS, OF HIS YOUNGER DAUGHTER, NINA.

HIS TROUBLED ELDER DAUGHTER, ZINA, WAS TO COMMIT SUICIDE IN 1933.

AT LAST TROTSKY WAS GIVEN THE CHOICE BETWEEN CEASING HIS POLITICAL ACTIVITY OR FACING EXPULSION FROM RUSSIA.

HE AND HIS WIFE DEPARTED THEIR NATIVE SOIL IN THE COMPANY OF THEIR ELDER SON, LEV SEDOV, AGE 22.

IN FEBRUARY 1929 THEY FIRST SETTLED IN ISTANBUL...

BLACK SEA

ISTANBUL

SEA OF MARMARA

PRINKIPO (BÜYÜKADA)

...BUT THE PRESENCE IN THE CITY OF FORMER WHITE ARMY OFFICERS COMPELLED THEM TO MOVE, FOR SECURITY REASONS, TO THE ISLAND OF PRINKIPO.

THERE TROTSKY'S POLITICAL ACTIVITY CONTINUED UNABATED.

HE FOUNDED THE PERIODICAL *BULLETIN OF THE OPPOSITION* (PUBLISHED IN PARIS), DEDICATED TO THE PERPETUATION OF LENINIST PRINCIPLES.

HE DECLARED THE LEFT OPPOSITION, AS HIS MOVEMENT NOW CALLED ITSELF, TO BE A FACTION OF THE THIRD COMMUNIST INTERNATIONAL (COMINTERN), FOUNDED BY LENIN IN 1919.

IN 1932 HE AND HIS WIFE AND SON WERE DEPRIVED BY STALIN'S GOVERNMENT OF THEIR SOVIET CITIZENSHIP.

LIFE ON THE ISLAND, WHILE NOT LUXURIOUS, WAS COMFORTABLE.

AN AVID HUNTER AND FISHERMAN, TROTSKY FOUND TIME TO INDULGE IN HIS FAVORITE PASTIMES.

IN 1933, ADOLF HITLER BECAME CHANCELLOR OF GERMANY.

THE GERMAN COMMUNIST PARTY CAPITULATED TO THE NEW LEADER, WHILE STALIN LOOKED ON WITH APPROVAL.

IN JUNE 1933, AFTER FOUR YEARS IN TURKEY, TROTSKY AND NATALIA WERE GRANTED VISAS TO RELOCATE IN FRANCE...

PARIS

ISTANBUL

...PERMISSION HAVING BEEN GIVEN BY THE LEFTIST REGIME OF PRIME MINISTER ÉDOUARD DALADIER, WITH THE PROVISO THAT TROTSKY ABSTAIN FROM POLITICAL ACTIVITY.

THEIR RESIDENCE IN FRANCE WAS A TURBULENT ONE. THEIR FIRST HOME, ON THE ATLANTIC COAST, BURNED TO THE GROUND.

THEY MOVED THEREAFTER FROM HOUSE TO HOUSE, NEVER SETTLING IN A PERMANENT ABODE. THE GOVERNMENT, FINDING TROTSKY A LIABILITY, REFUSED HIM PERMISSION TO RESIDE IN PARIS.

REALIZING THAT STALIN AND THE COMINTERN WERE HOPELESSLY CORRUPT, TROTSKY DECLARED THAT A FOURTH INTERNATIONAL WAS NECESSARY.

BUT WITH HIS SUPPORTERS SCATTERED AND NO LARGE ORGANIZATION AT HIS DISPOSAL, HE COULD DO LITTLE TO IMPLEMENT HIS IDEAS.

IN 1934 A RIGHT-WING GOVERNMENT CAME TO POWER IN FRANCE. FACED WITH HARASSMENT FROM FASCISTS AND STALINISTS ALIKE, AND FREQUENTLY BEDRIDDEN FROM HIS RECURRING ILLNESS, TROTSKY SOUGHT ISOLATION IN THE TOWN OF GRENOBLE.

IN JUNE 1935, HE AND NATALIA MOVED TO NORWAY, AT THE INVITATION OF THAT NATION'S NEWLY ELECTED SOCIAL DEMOCRATIC GOVERNMENT...

OSLO

PARIS

...AGAIN WITH THE STIPULATION THAT HE REFRAIN FROM REVOLUTIONARY ACTIVITY.

HE KEPT AT HIS WRITING, HOWEVER, SO OUTRAGING THE SOVIET GOVERNMENT THAT IT LODGED AN OFFICIAL PROTEST WITH THE NORWEGIANS.

THE RESULT WAS THAT HE WAS PLACED UNDER VIRTUAL HOUSE ARREST.

IN AUGUST 1936 MEMBERS OF THE FASCIST PARTY BROKE INTO THE TROTSKY HOME WHILE THE COUPLE WERE OUT...

...IN HOPES OF FINDING DOCUMENTS AND OTHER PROOF TO FORCE HIM OUT OF THE COUNTRY.

91

THAT SAME MONTH THE FIRST OF STALIN'S "SHOW TRIALS" OPENED IN MOSCOW, WITH THE FORMER LEADERS OF THE OPPOSITION—KAMENEV, ZINOVIEV, AND 14 OTHERS—CONDEMNED FOR TERRORISM AGAINST THE STATE.

ALL THE ACCUSED WERE COERCED INTO SIGNING CONFESSIONS AND GRANTED NO DEFENSE ATTORNEYS.

THE TRIALS WERE SCRIPTED IN DETAIL, DOWN TO THE FINAL AND INEVITABLE VERDICT OF GUILTY...

ВИНОВНЫЙ!

...AFTER WHICH ALL OF THEM WERE EXECUTED.

TROTSKY AND HIS SON LEV WERE LIKEWISE CHARGED, IN ABSENTIA, WITH CONSPIRACY TO OVERTHROW THE SOVIET GOVERNMENT.

BY THE END OF 1936 THE NORWEGIAN GOVERNMENT THOUGHT IT HAD SUFFICIENT EXCUSE TO EXPEL TROTSKY FROM THE COUNTRY.

HE AND NATALIA BOARDED A FREIGHTER...

...AND SAILED FOR MEXICO.

UPON DISEMBARKING AT THE PORT OF TAMPICO, THEY WERE WARMLY WELCOMED BY THE MEXICAN PRESIDENT, LÁZARO CÁRDENAS.

MEXICO'S MOST FAMOUS ARTISTIC COUPLE, DIEGO RIVERA AND FRIDA KAHLO, BOTH OF THEM ARDENT COMMUNISTS, WELCOMED THE EXILE...

...AND OPENED TO HIM AND NATALIA THEIR HOUSE, CASA AZUL, IN THE COYOACÁN SUBURB OF MEXICO CITY.

AT THE SECOND MOSCOW SHOW TRIAL, IN JANUARY 1937, TROTSKY AND HIS SON WERE FURTHER CHARGED AS BEING AGENTS OF WORLD FASCISM.

TROTSKY AT ONCE SET ABOUT TO CLEAR HIS NAME OF THIS AVALANCHE OF CHARGES.

AN INDEPENDENT COMMISSION OF INQUIRY, CHAIRED BY THE AMERICAN LIBERAL ACTIVIST JOHN DEWEY, WAS ORGANIZED.

THE COMMISSION MET IN MEXICO CITY AND TOOK TESTIMONY DURING APRIL.

NOT GUILTY!

IN SEPTEMBER ITS CONCLUSION WAS ANNOUNCED: STALIN'S SHOW TRIALS WERE TRAVESTIES OF JUSTICE; TROTSKY AND HIS SON WERE NOT GUILTY.

94

MEXICO DURING THESE YEARS WAS SCARCELY A REFUGE FOR TROTSKY FROM THE POLITICAL TURMOIL OF EUROPE.

THE MEXICAN COMMUNIST PARTY WAS IN A STRUGGLE BETWEEN ITS STALINISTS AND ITS TROTSKYISTS.

IN SEPTEMBER 1938 THE FOUNDING CONFERENCE OF THE FOURTH INTERNATIONAL WAS HELD IN EUROPE...

...PROMOTED BY TROTSKY AND HIS ALLIES AS AN INTERNATIONALIST ALTERNATIVE TO STALIN'S COMINTERN.

THE CIVIL WAR THEN RAGING IN SPAIN WAS A STAGE FOR THE POLITICAL RIFTS OF THE WORLD AT LARGE.

THE GOVERNMENT OF THE REPUBLIC, SUPPORTED BY THE SOVIET UNION, WAS WEAKENED BY THE SPLIT WITHIN THE COMMUNIST PARTY, ENABLING THE ULTIMATE VICTORY OF FRANCISCO FRANCO'S RIGHT-WING FORCES, SUPPORTED BY HITLER'S NAZI REGIME.

THE INFAMOUS AGREEMENT BETWEEN HITLER AND THE EUROPEAN POWERS AT MUNICH LED TO THE GERMAN TAKEOVER OF CZECHOSLOVAKIA...

...AND A MAJOR STEP TOWARD ANOTHER WORLD WAR.

ALSO THAT YEAR, THE TROTSKYS LEARNED OF THE MYSTERIOUS DEATH, IN A PARIS HOSPITAL, OF THEIR ELDER SON, LEV. ALTHOUGH THE OFFICIAL CONCLUSION WAS DEATH BY NATURAL CAUSES, TROTSKY SUSPECTED THAT STALIN'S SECRET POLICE WERE BEHIND IT.

(THE COUPLE'S YOUNGER, NONPOLITICAL SON, SERGEI, HAD BEEN ARRESTED THE PREVIOUS YEAR AND WAS TO DIE IN A CONCENTRATION CAMP.)

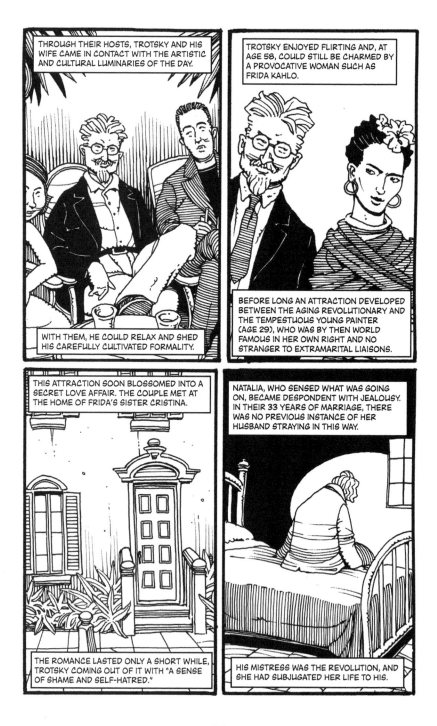

THROUGH THEIR HOSTS, TROTSKY AND HIS WIFE CAME IN CONTACT WITH THE ARTISTIC AND CULTURAL LUMINARIES OF THE DAY.

WITH THEM, HE COULD RELAX AND SHED HIS CAREFULLY CULTIVATED FORMALITY.

TROTSKY ENJOYED FLIRTING AND, AT AGE 58, COULD STILL BE CHARMED BY A PROVOCATIVE WOMAN SUCH AS FRIDA KAHLO.

BEFORE LONG AN ATTRACTION DEVELOPED BETWEEN THE AGING REVOLUTIONARY AND THE TEMPESTUOUS YOUNG PAINTER (AGE 29), WHO WAS BY THEN WORLD FAMOUS IN HER OWN RIGHT AND NO STRANGER TO EXTRAMARITAL LIAISONS.

THIS ATTRACTION SOON BLOSSOMED INTO A SECRET LOVE AFFAIR. THE COUPLE MET AT THE HOME OF FRIDA'S SISTER CRISTINA.

THE ROMANCE LASTED ONLY A SHORT WHILE, TROTSKY COMING OUT OF IT WITH "A SENSE OF SHAME AND SELF-HATRED."

NATALIA, WHO SENSED WHAT WAS GOING ON, BECAME DESPONDENT WITH JEALOUSY. IN THEIR 33 YEARS OF MARRIAGE, THERE WAS NO PREVIOUS INSTANCE OF HER HUSBAND STRAYING IN THIS WAY.

HIS MISTRESS WAS THE REVOLUTION, AND SHE HAD SUBJUGATED HER LIFE TO HIS.

TROTSKY'S ULTIMATE BREAK WITH DIEGO RIVERA (WHO WAS UNAWARE OF THE AFFAIR) WAS ALONG POLITICAL LINES.

THE LEGENDARY MURALIST ADMIRED TROTSKY AND CONSIDERED HIMSELF A DISCIPLE.

HE HAD, AFTER ALL, IMMORTALIZED THE REVOLUTIONARY IN HIS WORK.

WORKERS OF THE W

MAN, CONTROLLER OF THE UNIVERSE (1934), PALACIO DE BELLAS ARTES, MEXICO CITY.

RIVERA WAS INTENT ON BECOMING THE LEADER OF THE MEXICAN TROTSKYISTS. BUT THE TWO MEN FOUND THEMSELVES DIVIDED OVER ISSUES OF TEMPERAMENT.

TROTSKY FOUND THE ARTIST DISORGANIZED, NEGLIGENT, AND LACKING IN DEDICATION.

RIVERA FOUND TROTSKY SELF-SERVNG AND INFLEXIBLE.

BY JANUARY 1939 RIVERA HAD QUIT THE FOURTH INTERNATIONAL AND THE TROTSKYS HAD QUIT CASA AZUL.

97

THEY MOVED TO A HOUSE ON AVENIDA VIENA IN COYOACÁN. IN MARCH OF THAT YEAR STALIN ORDERED THE "EXECUTION" OF TROTSKY, AND HE WAS PLACED UNDER GUARD.

THE SECOND WORLD WAR BEGAN IN SEPTEMBER, WITH GERMANY'S INVASION OF POLAND.

THIS WAS ALLOWED BY STALIN BECAUSE HE AND HITLER HAD SIGNED A NONAGGRESSION PACT.

ON MAY 24, 1940, 20 AGENTS OF THE SOVIET SECRET POLICE, LED BY THE MEXICAN PAINTER DAVID ALFARO SIQUEIROS, INVADED THE TROTSKY HOME WITH MACHINE GUNS.

MORE THAN 80 ROUNDS WERE FIRED INTO THE COUPLE'S BEDROOM, BUT THEY WERE NOT HIT. THE ATTACKERS WERE DRIVEN BACK BY SECURITY GUARDS.

AFTER THIS, THE HOUSE WAS TURNED INTO A FORTRESS, WITH REINFORCED DOORS AND WINDOWS...

...AND TRIPLE THE NUMBER OF GUARDS.

THESE MEASURES CAME TOO LATE.

A SPANISH ÉMIGRÉ NAMED RAMÓN MERCADER, A STALINIST AGENT POSING AS A FRIVOLOUS NONPOLITICAL BUSINESSMAN, HAD BY THIS TIME INSINUATED HIMSELF INTO TROTSKY'S ENTOURAGE.

HIS SUPPOSED LOVE AFFAIR WITH ONE OF TROTSKY'S SECRETARIES GAVE HIM ACCESS TO THE HOUSE.

HE MADE DETAILED MAPS OF THE PREMISES, WHICH GUIDED THE ASSASSINS OF THE MAY 24 INVASION.

HE CHARMED THE HOUSEHOLD AND MADE HIMSELF USEFUL, DRIVING NATALIA AND HER FRIENDS ON SHOPPING EXCURSIONS.

THE PRETENSE OF AN EMERGING POLITICAL CONSCIOUSNESS GAINED HIM ACCESS TO TROTSKY...

...WHOM HE PEPPERED WITH QUESTIONS AND FLATTERY.

ON AUGUST 20, 1940, ARMED WITH A MOUNTAIN CLIMBER'S ICE AX, MERCADER CAME TO TROTSKY'S STUDY.

HE ASKED THE OLDER MAN TO READ AN ARTICLE THAT HE HAD WRITTEN AND, WHILE HE WAS DOING SO, DEALT HIM A HEAVY BLOW TO THE HEAD.

TROTSKY LEAPED UP AND, WITH A FINAL BURST OF ENERGY, TRIED TO ATTACK HIS ASSASSIN. BUT MERCADER PUSHED HIM TO THE FLOOR.

TAKEN TO A LOCAL HOSPITAL, TROTSKY LINGERED FOR ANOTHER DAY...

...AND DIED ON THE EVENING OF AUGUST 21.

OVER THE NEXT SEVERAL DAYS, HUGE CROWDS FILED BY HIS COFFIN.

HIS FUNERAL PROCESSION PACKED THE STREETS OF MEXICO CITY.

TODAY HIS STUDY IS PRESERVED MUCH AS IT WAS DURING HIS LIFETIME. AT AGE 60, HE HAD SPENT MORE THAN HALF HIS LIFE EITHER IN PRISON OR IN EXILE FROM HIS NATIVE LAND.

LEON TROTSKY

HIS ASHES ARE BURIED, ALONG WITH THOSE OF HIS WIFE (WHO DIED IN 1962), UNDER AN IMPOSING MARKER IN THE COYOACÁN NEIGHBORHOOD WHERE HE SPENT HIS LAST YEARS.

FURTHER READING

Deutscher, Isaac. *Trotsky: The Prophet Armed*. Brooklyn, N.Y.: Verso, 2003.

Deutscher, Isaac. *Trotsky: The Prophet Unarmed*. Brooklyn, N.Y.: Verso, 2003.

Deutscher, Isaac. *Trotsky: The Prophet Outcast*. Brooklyn, N.Y.: Verso, 2003.

Marx, Karl, and Friedrich Engels. *The Marx-Engels Reader*. New York: W. W. Norton, 1978.

Pipes, Richard, ed. *The Unknown Lenin: From the Secret Archive*. New Haven: Yale University Press, 1999.

Riasanovsky, Nicholas V., and Mark Steinberg. *A History of Russia: Combined Volume*. New York: Oxford University Press, 2004.

Thatcher, Ian D. *Trotsky*. New York: Routledge, 2002.

Trotsky, Leon. *My Life*. Atlanta: Pathfinder Press, 1970.

Volkogonov, Dmitri. *Trotsky: The Eternal Revolutionary*. New York: Free Press, 2007.

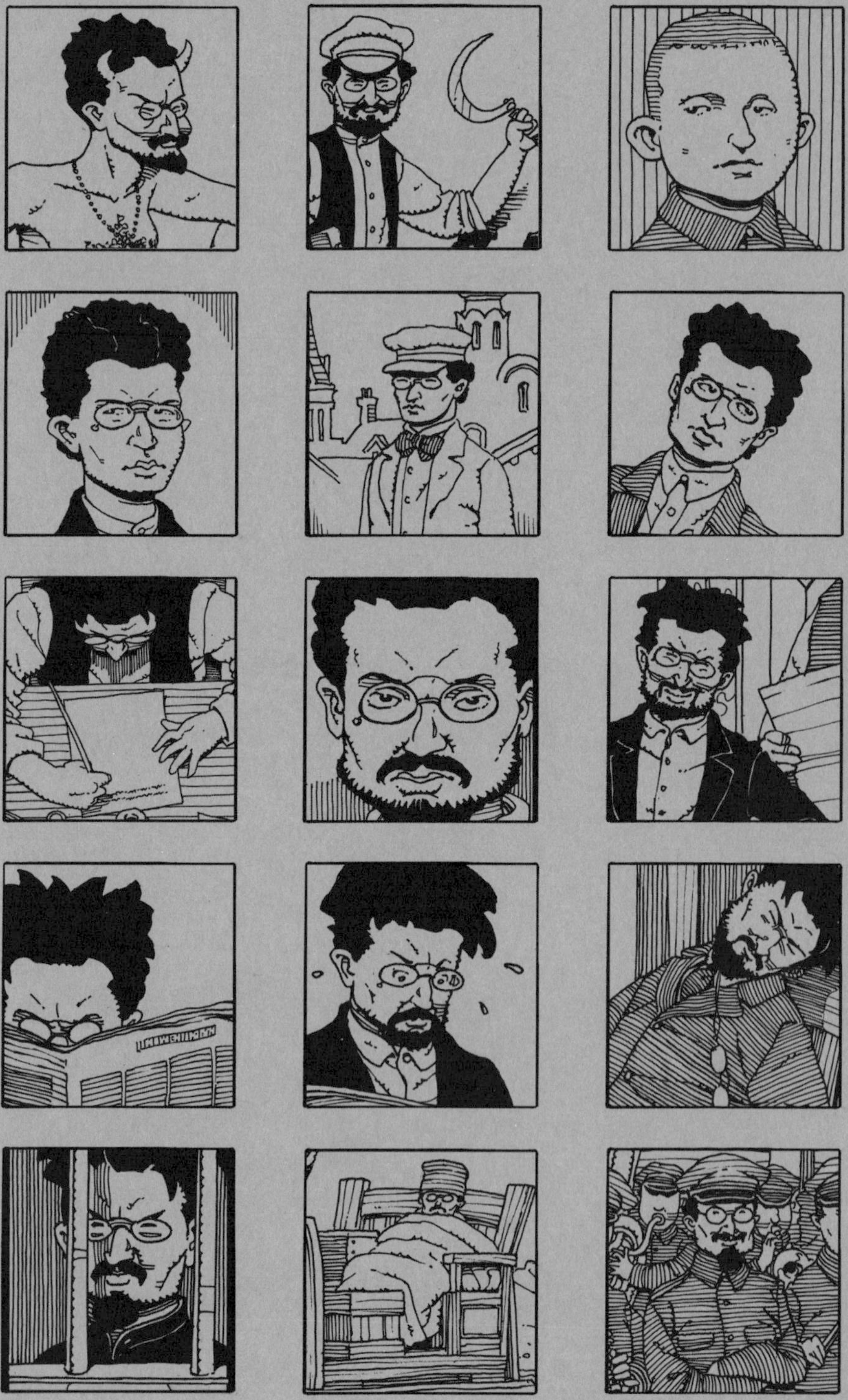